presents

Maha Reiki®
Level 1 Manual

In Depth Reiki Training for Our Times

Donna Lambdin, Ph.D.
Ron Goodwin, Ph.D.

For online training webinar information,
please visit www.mahamethods.com

ACKNOWLEDGMENTS

Donna wishes to thank her guardian angel who is referred to as Grandmother, for reminding her of her sacred contract. This manual is in part the fulfillment of that contract. Donna also wants to express her gratitude to Lorrie Richmond for introducing her to Reiki and for being a wonderful friend and confidant. She also wants to thank her mentor Rosalie and her Reiki Master Teachers for their teachings, patience, and wisdom.

Many others have helped us on our journey, especially our Kundalini Yoga Instructor Shamsher.

Many thanks to Elizabeth Klein, Isaiah T. Miles, and Lisa Zepeda for being the Reiki models. We thank Barbara DuBois for the cover design and page layout, along with her graphic illustrations; Lisa Lombardo for her cover and chapter header artwork; and Cori Johnson for helping us with our computers and technology.

The support and encouragement from our friends, students, clients, fellow Reiki Masters and Practitioners has been most helpful.

It was our privilege to meet an incredible artist while we were in Kona, Hawaii: Francene Hart. She has allowed us to use a few of her prints in our manual. For this we are forever grateful. Her website is *www.francenehart.com* and her mailing address is P.O. Box 900, Honaunau, HI 96726.

So much Love, Light, and Blessings to all on your Reiki journey.

Donna Lambdin and Ron Goodwin

DISCLAIMER

The purpose of this training manual is to assist Maha Reiki® Master Teachers and their students in understanding and learning Maha Reiki®. Maha Reiki® cannot be learned and practiced without receiving an attunement from a qualified Maha Reiki® Master Teacher.

The information in this manual is not medical advice and is not intended as a substitute for seeking medical attention.

TABLE OF CONTENTS

Foreword 1

Code of Ethics 2

Welcome Letter 3

How I Discovered Reiki 4

Illustration: Reiki *Kanji* Symbols 6

History 7

Illustration: Master Lineage 10

Flower of Life/Sacred Geometry 11

Five Precepts 12

Illustration: *Wheels of Light* by Francene Hart 13

Chakras 15

Chakra Balancing Meditation 25

Illustration: Spinning Chakras 27

Illustration: Auric Field Layers 28

Auric Field 29

Aura Strengthening Exercise 31

Reiki: What It Is and How It Works 32

Illustration: *Receiving* by Francene Hart 39

Meditation for Attunement 41

Reiki Attunement 42

Hand Positions for Self Reiki 44

Reiki Session 48

Hand Positions for Treating Others 51

Hand Positions for Seated Reiki 61

Illustration: Anatomy for Reiki (Front View) 64

Illustration: Anatomy for Reiki (Back View) 65

Client Information Form 66

Daily Practice 67

Sacred Space 69

Reiki Circle 70

Illustration: Domesticated Animal Chakras 71

Animal Reiki 73

Bibliography 75

FOREWORD

The time is now!

In this current time of conscious development, fresh tools for teaching and learning are needed to assist in this journey. Many books have been written on Reiki, energetic, vibrational, and spiritual healing. Current mainstream magazines have recently published articles on a variety of alternative energetic healing methods, thus bringing the awareness of these methods to the public eye. The overview of these articles is sparking interest and awakening many people.

As individuals begin to awaken, many feel lost as to where to begin to find answers. The internet provides an immense amount of information, but where does a person go to find actual training? Hands on instruction is needed for Reiki and many other alternative healing methods. Many attunements and empowerments, unlocking the keys to raise vibrational consciousness, are passed on from teacher to student, in person.

Understanding, experiencing, and continuing guidance and support are important when a person is just beginning and continues to practice Reiki. Person to person contact fulfills this movement and growth. Contact with your Reiki Master Teacher and other Reiki practitioners can be extremely supportive and comforting.

Maha Reiki® has developed over many years of practicing and teaching the Usui and Tibetan styles of Reiki. These teachings are the foundation of this practice. Maha is a Sanskrit word meaning "Great". New methods and ways of understanding the power of this amazing Reiki energy have grown and developed with daily practice and sessions with countless clients and students. "Do not minimize," these were the words spoken to me by Spirit. This guidance has assisted in my growth, continuing development, understanding, and teaching others advanced techniques with the Maha Reiki® energy.

This Maha Reiki® Level 1 manual provides more advanced techniques and methods to empower and support the growth of your Reiki practice. This manual does not replace the need for the student to receive an in-person attunement from a qualified Maha Reiki® Master Teacher.

The time is now! Unlock your energetic, infinite potential!
Many blessings on your journey!

Donna Lambdin
Maha Reiki® Master Teacher

MAHA REIKI®
CODE OF ETHICS

The following are the basic operating principles of Maha Reiki® and our Code of Ethics. All students, practitioners, and teachers should keep these principles in mind as they practice and teach Maha Reiki®.

1. Show gratitude for the gift of Reiki and for all fellow students, practitioners, and teachers, regardless of school or lineage.

2. Be honest, show respect, and have integrity in all you do.

3. Treat all information from clients, students, practitioners, and teachers in a confidential manner.

4. Recognize that Reiki works in conjunction with other forms of medical care. Never diagnose or prescribe medications. Refer clients other health care professionals when appropriate.

5. Always act in a professional manner and maintain a professional image.

6. Use common sense and seek the advice of experienced Maha Reiki® professionals when in doubt.

Welcome to Maha Reiki® Level I Training!

Your journey has led you to this moment of moving forward into higher light and vibration. With this first level of Maha Reiki® training, you will be embracing a new opening on your path of life force energy.

Maha Reiki® is a Reiki system which enhances the combination of Usui Reiki, which was brought forward by Mikao Usui, and Tibetan Reiki. Refer to the History section for more information.

Walking this journey with you, either as a direct teacher or through another Reiki Master Teacher, is a great honor for me. My heart soars to greater heights as I witness the growth and understanding that you accomplish and allow to continue...unfolding your talents, gifts, and connection to infinite Divine, compassionate healing energy.

The brilliance and purity of the Divine energy, highest light, which you continue to embrace and integrate into your daily practice, can lead you to places you cannot even imagine. For if you could imagine, you are putting limitations on yourself.

Learning to trust, take each day as the gift it truly is. Flow without fear, worry, or anger. Fill with gratitude and honor. Allow your Spirit to soar to heights unimaginable, no limits, no barriers, only truth. Each day is new. Each day carries you closer to your highest consciousness and beyond.

Welcome to this class. Welcome to the unconditional love that wraps you in a cocoon of light, infinite...

Sat Nam, Namaste,
Donna Lambdin
Maha Reiki® Master Teacher

HOW I DISCOVERED REIKI

I have been fortunate all of my life to have my personal connection with my guardian angel. From my earliest memories, I saw my angel, felt its presence, knew I was not alone and always felt protected.

I have always found great joy in all that nature and the elements have to provide. At the age of two, my family could not keep me out of the water. This was a time before neighbors had fences. I was always running across the yard and jumping into the neighbor's pool. Being in water was natural, comforting and joyful. When my family lived on an island in Florida, I was allowed to go across the street, and swim alone at the beach. The dolphins would come and swim with me. I thought this was normal and was experienced by everyone. The joy of swimming with schools of fish and having the dolphins nearby and so close we could touch, was pure joy. Being in the forest or in gardens also has always brought me peace and joy. Yes, I talk to trees, plant Devas, fairies, elementals…this was always my secret, as being raised Southern Baptist in the deep south did not encourage speaking of these things!

At the age of five, I began dancing. Pure freedom of expression and movement was sheer joy. Dancing was my passion. At the age of 15, my ballet teacher moved away and left her studio in my care. This is when financial independence came into my life. I became the ballet teacher in my small town of 40,000 people. This included choreographing two performances a year for my students, working with the little theater productions, and private entertainment at retirement and nursing homes.

At the age of 25, I moved to the Pacific Northwest. For the next 28 years of my life, I worked with interior plants in commercial office buildings. Visiting 65 different businesses a week, some having 12 to 500 employees, I cared for hundreds of plants and spoke with thousands of people. As I worked on the plants, I noticed the discomfort of many of the employees. I began giving tips to assist their comfort in their working environment, developing a corporate wellness program. This included, breathing, stretching, drinking water, and many more tips to enhance their comfort level. As my own strenuous work began to take a toll on my physical body, I knew I needed to change professions. Not having a clue as to what that would be, I started asking my guardian angel for guidance and assistance.

In the year 2000, I was guided to take a two-year vibrational medicine course. During the second month of this course, my guardian angel, who I call Grandmother, woke me up in the middle of the night. She was never a solid figure, nor a ghost, but a translucent being with flowing hair and dress. Grandmother Spirit pointed her finger right into my face. These were her words: *You made a sacred contract before you came into this body. I am here to remind you what that contract is. You will touch people and help them to heal. You are going to live a very long time and you are going to touch millions of people. Remember this: Do not minimize, the energy is infinite.* As she started to fade I exclaimed "I will, but you have to help me, help me!" I take the words *sacred contract* seriously. This is more important to me than anything else in this lifetime. It has guided me from that moment on.

Over the next month my training began to unfold as three new doors opened, introducing me to three new teachers and mentors. A friend, and spiritual confidant, in one of my plant accounts introduced me to Reiki. She gave me the phone number of her Reiki Master, who lived in another state. I called, we connected, and my Level 1 Reiki training happened within the month. Through my vibrational medicine class, I was introduced to my Kundalini yoga teacher. Another friend introduced me to his sister, who introduced me to their mother, a medicine woman recognized by all First Nations in North America. The phrase "ask and you shall receive," can and does happen when the asking is in one's highest good. I was very blessed.

Reiki changed my life immediately. The increased vibrational energy that flowed through my hands daily enhanced all of my work and everything that I touched. My intuitiveness increased. I began to "see" more clearly. All of my senses were heightened. In my plant accounts, employees asked me to place my hands on their shoulders, neck, or head for pain and stress relief. I was doing as much Reiki as I was plant care in these accounts. After a year, people began asking for full Reiki sessions after work.

My original Reiki Master Teacher was of the old school. She taught me one could not practice Reiki on others as a practitioner until they were Level 2 trained. I called her and asked if she would come to do my training. She came and we had a three-day intensive training at my cabin in the Quinault rain forest. Being of the old school training, I was not allowed to write anything down. The memorizing of the symbols was highly important!

I began seeing private clients, after work and on the weekends. During this time, clients began asking me to teach them Reiki. I called my Reiki Master once again. After learning she would not teach the Masters level, I searched for another teacher. I found a Master Teacher class being taught in Oregon, two weeks later, just before my birthday! Since that time, I have been honored to teach thousands of people the gift of Reiki. Many are now highly qualified Master Teachers! It is a blessing to me to know that everyone each of my students touch, I also touch, following the journey of my sacred contract.

On the following page are the two commonly used Japanese *Kanji* Symbols which represent Reiki. They can be found in Reiki literature, at historic sites, and on carved meditation stones.

Donna Lambdin
Maha Reiki® Master Teacher

JAPANESE REIKI KANJI SYMBOLS

Pre-1940   *Modern - commonly used*

HISTORY

It is a common belief that Reiki was discovered by Mikao Usui, on his 21-day fast and meditation on Mount Kurama, near Kyoto, Japan. I believe that Reiki is a part of all of us and was taught to all in early civilizations. Over time, it was lost and now has been rediscovered for the benefit of all mankind.

The traditional Reiki story can be found in many books with some variations. Dr. Mikao Usui was born August 15, 1865, in a village located near the present day city of Nagoya, Japan. There are various accounts that Usui Sensei, as he was known by many, attended a Buddhist school at an early age and developed a keen interest in health and healing, using life energy. He found that using life energy for healing work depleted the practitioner's own life energy and wondered if it was possible to perform the healing work without depleting one's own energy. Over the years, Usui traveled to Europe and China and studied various subjects including religion, psychology, and medicine. He also was able to make social connections which would help him to become a successful businessman.

Around 1914, Usui began to have personal problems and his business was going downhill. He traveled to Mount Kurama, where he had spent time in his early childhood. He enrolled in a 21-day Tendai Buddhist training course. It is believed that the training included fasting, meditation, chanting, and prayer. On the 21st day, being in an extremely weakened state, Usui experienced a life-changing event.

The story I was told by my first Reiki Master was the following: As Usui gazed at the stars in meditation, weak and near death, a star began to move, coming closer and closer to Usui until it flew into his third eye. At this point, he fell into unconsciousness. During this time of near death, his spirit journeyed to a higher realm of consciousness where he was given the tools of hands-on healing by higher vibrational beings, along with the Reiki Symbols. As he awoke from this experience, he was filled with vitality, a higher spiritual connection, and awareness of flowing vibrational energy.

There is also a theory that Reiki is much older than Usui's discovery. In Diane Stein's book, *Essential Reiki: A Complete Guide To An Ancient Healing Art* (1995), she discusses information that she received from a psychic concerning the origin of Reiki. The psychic, Laurel Steinhice, states: "Reiki originated with the planet that also brought the many-armed gods and goddesses to Earth, the root culture of what became pre-patriarchal India. The Indian god we know today as Shiva, female at that time, was responsible for bringing Reiki here, and s/he wants to be remembered for the gift. When the human body for this planet was designed, Reiki was incorporated into genetic coding as a birthright of all people," (8). While this information is unverified, it is important to consider.

Over the next several years, Usui used his healing ability to help others, especially the poor. In 1922, he moved to Tokyo and started a healing center. Two other healing centers were also opened. In 1923, Tokyo was devastated by the great Kanto earthquake. More than 140,000 people died in the quake and the city was in shambles. Thousands of people were left homeless, injured and sick.

Usui began treating as many people as he could. Due to great demand, he built a bigger facility in Nakano, Tokyo. It is said that he trained over 2,000 students and 21 Reiki Masters in his lifetime. Usui died of a stroke in 1926 while teaching in Fukuyama. Reiki students in Japan referred to Usui as Usui Sensei. *Sensei* means honorable teacher, master.

Chujiro Hayashi

It was during the earthquake period that Usui met Chujiro Hayashi, a retired doctor and Naval officer. Hayashi became a student and received his Master training from Usui in 1925. Hayashi trained many Reiki practitioners, both men and women, and is said to have trained around 16 Reiki Masters. Per the request of Usui Sensei, he opened a healing clinic in Tokyo and had practitioners work in groups on clients, many of whom stayed at the clinic during their treatments. Hayashi also had his practitioners make house calls to those who were unable to visit the clinic. He created a healing guide for which hand positions worked best on the body for specific symptoms. Hayashi Sensei developed new styles of Reiki, teaching, and attunement methods. He passed in 1940.

Hawayo Takata

A Japanese woman born on Kauai, Hawaii in 1900, Hawayo Takata would be the person responsible for bringing Reiki to the West. At the age of 35, a mother of two daughters, Takata became a widow. When her sister also passed, Takata felt it was her duty to take the news back to her parents in Japan. At that time she was very ill, diagnosed with appendicitis, lung issues, gallstones, and an abdominal tumor. Takata sought medical care in Japan.

While being prepped for surgery in a Tokyo hospital, she heard a voice that the surgery was not necessary and that there was a better way. She asked the surgeon if there was another way for her to heal and he told her about Hayashi's Reiki clinic. The surgeon's sister had been healed at the clinic and had also received Reiki training. The sister took Takata to the clinic where she stayed for four months. She received treatments over the four months and got progressively better. By the end of the treatment period she was well.

The healing experience made a significant impression on Takata. She became Hayashi's student and after letters on her behalf from the Japanese medical community, she received her First and Second Degree training from Hayashi. In those days it was very rare for a woman to receive this type of training.

In 1937, Takata returned to Hawaii to establish a Reiki practice. In 1938, Takata received her Master/ Teacher training from Hayashi when he came to visit her in Hawaii. Records indicate that she was one of 13 Reiki Masters trained by Hayashi. Takata opened several Reiki clinics in Hawaii and kept the practice alive. After WWII she traveled to the U.S. mainland, Canada, and other parts of the world, teaching and giving treatments. Takata changed her method of speaking and teaching to match the societal consciousness of the different groups and countries in which she taught. By 1970, she began training Reiki Masters. Her philosophy would be considered "old school" by today's standards. Her fee for a weekend Master's Class was reported to be $10,000.

It is thought that the high fee was her way of creating respect for Reiki. She also felt that there should be due consideration for all Reiki services because it would not be respected or valued if there was not an exchange of monetary value.

She did not allow her students to take notes, everything had to be memorized. Because of this method of teaching there are variations in the symbols. There were also variations in the length and content of the classes. She also believed that a student should only have one Reiki Master/Teacher. Records show that she trained 22 Masters.

Reiki Evolving after Takata

While we can be grateful for Takata's contribution to Reiki, there are others who also made significant contributions.

Iris Ishikura, Takata's cousin and student, worked with energetic healing and used Tibetan symbols in her practice. She taught two Masters: her daughter Ruby and Arthur Robertson. Robertson taught many students, using the both the Usui and Raku Rei Reiki systems. He also worked with Iris Ishikura and in the early 1980s they included the chakra system, the Hui Yin breath, Fire Dragon, the Johre Symbol, and the Tibetan symbols. Both Iris Ishikura and Robertson are noted for breaking tradition with the restrictions that Takata had placed on the practice. It is believed that both helped bring Reiki forward to the masses by making the classes affordable.

Another student, Barbara Ray, made certain changes and taught what she called the Radiance Technique. She formed the Radiance Technique International Association, Inc.

Other individuals who were not direct students of Takata have made major contributions to the Reiki practice. They include William Rand, who teaches Usui/Tibetan Reiki and Karuna® Reiki. Rand also founded the International Center for Reiki Training and has been instrumental in offering quality Reiki training. Kathleen Milner changed the original Raku Kei Reiki system of attunements and added new symbols. This system claims to connect through Buddha to the source of all healing.

There are many forms of Reiki that stem from the core teachings of Usui Sensei. Many masters are teaching and evolving the practice as the needs of the population grow. It is interesting to note that mainstream publishers, like Time and Life, have come out with special alternative healing magazines. It is an indicator that the public is ready for alternatives such as Reiki. The Reiki energy practiced with pure, highest intention and spiritual connection, can be an important tool for each person who decides to embrace the energy.

To fully appreciate the power of Reiki, it is important to have an understanding of both chakras and the auric field, which we will cover in depth in later chapters.

Master Lineage

Dr. Mikao Usui

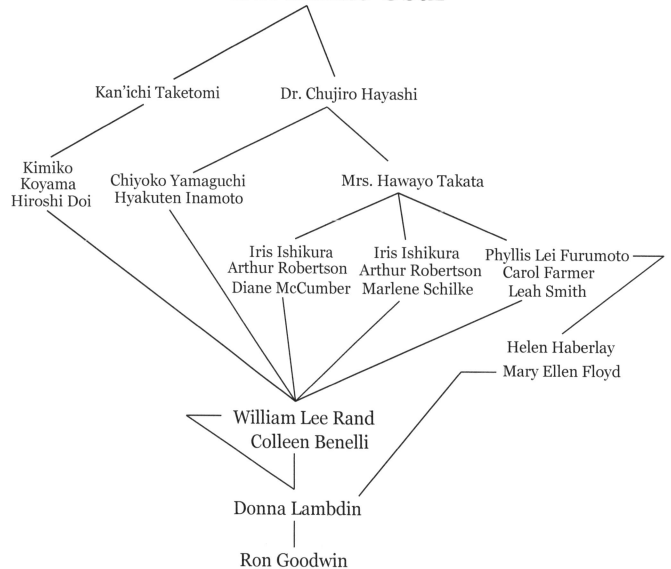

Kan'ichi Taketomi   Dr. Chujiro Hayashi

Kimiko
Koyama   Chiyoko Yamaguchi   Mrs. Hawayo Takata
Hiroshi Doi   Hyakuten Inamoto

Iris Ishikura   Iris Ishikura   Phyllis Lei Furumoto
Arthur Robertson   Arthur Robertson   Carol Farmer
Diane McCumber   Marlene Schilke   Leah Smith

Helen Haberlay

Mary Ellen Floyd

William Lee Rand
Colleen Benelli

Donna Lambdin

Ron Goodwin

FLOWER OF LIFE/SACRED GEOMETRY

The "Flower of Life" can be found in all major religions. This image is thousands of years old and can be found embedded in ancient sacred sites around the world.

The symbol mathematically contains all knowledge, all energy, all conscious thought, and structures that form the building blocks of life. Many say it contains the vibration of the Creator and through this symbol, can communicate directly.

The Flower of Life contains a sacred power which activates energy coding within your mind, assisting you to access higher vibrational presence.

Within this geometric image can be found the Platonic Solids which are mathematically the building blocks of the Universe. They form the basis of all life, language, music, and conscious thought.

THE FIVE PRECEPTS

Usui Sensei taught his students to place their hands together at their heart, morning and night, and repeat five precepts/principles. There are several similar interpretations of these precepts.
The following are the ones we are drawn to chant:

Just for today release anger

Just for today release worries

Earn your living honestly

Express gratitude

Be kind to every living thing

Repeating these precepts out loud, from your heart, can remind you, bring you joy in the moment, and carry you through your day with love!

Francene Hart

CHAKRAS

To better understand Reiki energetic and vibrational healing it is important to understand the chakra system. The word *chakra* comes from the Sanskrit language of India. It means *wheel*, and references centers of energy and awareness that are within each person. The chakras are energetic centers or portals into our energetic system that support our life force and life energy. For thousands of years, many cultures around the world have acknowledged the presence of energetic doors or wheels that determine our health within our physical body. Many believe we have seven major chakras within our body, along with many other chakras throughout the body. Traditional sources speak of up to 88,000 chakras.

We will be discussing nine chakras, the seven primary chakras as well as the earth chakra and the star chakra. These dictate the health of all of the other chakras. Each chakra is associated with a level of consciousness. As chakras open, a deeper level of understanding is achieved.

An understanding of the chakras is important, as stated by William Lee Rand in the book *The Spirit of Reiki: The Complete Handbook of the Reiki System* (2009), "The chakras are a part of the subtle energy system and play an important role in health and healing. Understanding them can be helpful when giving Reiki treatments. Blocks and negative energy are sometimes lodged in the chakras and, if present, need to be released in order for healing to take place" (83). There are a variety of ways that the blockages can be detected.

It is believed that the holy men and seers of ancient India, through their meditation, sensitivity, and yoga practice, directed their power within and discovered the chakra system. It is noted that while the chakra system has its origin in India, similar teachings are found in many cultures around the world. Kalashatra Govinda, in her book *A Handbook of Chakra Healing: Spiritual Practice for Health, Harmony, and Inner Peace* (2002), states: "Although we have the yoga tradition to thank for transmitting the teaching on the chakras, the phenomenon of the chakras has been recognized in many other cultures as well. The first reference to chakras is found in the Vedas, the most ancient religious texts of India, which date from around 1500 B.C.E. In the Upanishads, which comprise the esoteric parts of the Vedas, specific mention is made of techniques for activating the chakras" (9).

It is believed that the body contains seven main chakras, arranged from the base of the spine to the top of the head. They are thought to be spinning, funnel-shaped vortexes/portals in the subtle energy system. Some have also described the chakras as lotus blossoms, open flowers, and miniature suns. They influence cells, organs, thoughts, feelings, and the hormone system. They absorb external energies from the environment, plants, other people, as well as the sun, moon, and the entire cosmos. They allow cosmic energy to radiate from within and act as miniature suns. The energy is made available for processing physical, mental, emotional, and spiritual energies.

The chakras spin like wheels, funneling energy. On the front of the body they spin clockwise, addressing current issues and energy. On the back, they spin counterclockwise and represent issues and energy from the past. The chakras in the front need to spin in sync with each other to be in balance and to have energy flow freely from the root earth chakra to the star chakra above the head. The chakras in the back need to do the same. The front and back chakras, as their energies meet in the central core of your body, need to also spin in sync together. Then the flow from the earth chakra to the star chakra can open the connection. All the chakras meeting in the central core will flow and be in balance as all the spins become one. Balance is achieved!

When your chakras do not flow together in sync, it is like driving your car with different air pressure in all four tires. Your vehicle will eventually become out of balance and the different systems will begin to suffer. So it is within your own inner wheels of light, your chakras, and your organs. Any congestion in a chakra can slow or block the entire process of flow and balance. Life traumas, programming, and experiences that are being held in the sluggish chakras can be addressed, healed through vibration with forgiveness, acceptance as a learning experience, and released with love and blessings. This does not mean accepting actions as being right, but being willing to learn the lesson from the experience and releasing the energetic ties to that action so you are free to move forward in your life!

Anodea Judith, in her book *Wheels of Life, A User's Guide To The Chakra System* (2010), gives this explanation: "Chakras are organizing centers for the reception, assimilation, and transmission of life energies. Our chakras as core centers, form the coordinating network of our complicated mind/body system. From instinctual behavior to consciously planned strategies, from emotions to artistic creations, the chakras are the master programs that govern our life, loves, learning, and illumination. As seven vibratory modalities, the chakras form a mythical Rainbow Bridge, a connecting channel linking Heaven and Earth, mind and body, spirit and matter, past and future. As we spin through the tumultuous times of our present era, the chakras act as gears turning the spiral of evolution, drawing us ever onward toward the still untapped frontiers of consciousness and its infinite potential" (4).

Root Chakra

The first chakra, or *root chakra*, lies at the base of your tailbone. It vibrates to the color red, to the musical note C, and to the chant word LAM (pronounced *LOM*, like *mom*). This is where the fight or flight survival reactions and instincts live. The ability to be grounded, to feel at home in your body, is found here. The root chakra controls your colon, elimination, and lower body extremities. When you have issues affecting your lower vertebrae, bowels, bones, legs, and feet, this is where the congestion rests. The feelings of being shaky, ungrounded, fearful, or lost are also associated with the root chakra.

This chakra is home of the *kundalini*, which means "serpent power." In her book, Kalashatra Govinda discusses the kundalini: "In ancient India, the dominant interpretation of kundalini was that it is a coiled serpent that sleeps in the root chakra at the base of the spinal column. When the kundalini is awakened, it climbs up the spinal column through the sushumna channel. As it travels, it activates and binds together all the chakras one after the other. Kundalini reaches its goal when it arrives at the crown chakra. The main theme of the kundalini theory is that of self-development. Kundalini is nimble, as fast as lightning, and flexible. It stands as an ancient symbol for the enormous potential for growth that every person has" (202).

I have met people who are very ungrounded and are out of their body most of the time. Their spirit does not recognize or possibly accept the physical body that they have chosen for this lifetime. Feeling the daily vibration of the earth is very important for personal grounding. The earth's vibration shifts daily, due to the rotation of our entire solar system. In addition, we are constantly being energetically exposed to new vibrations from our universe moving past stars and galaxies and other cosmic influences, such as sunspots, that it has not been exposed to in thousands of years. These vibrational influences affect both the earth and us sometimes in a positive way, sometimes in a negative way. The ability and awareness to change and ground daily into these new subtle vibrations is an important factor for each of us. As we fully ground our spirit into our physical bodies, this action allows us to soar into higher levels of consciousness.

A young man came to me for a Reiki session. He was ungrounded and unable to stay in his body. He was very flighty, to say the least. This situation was affecting everything in his life: his relationships with family and friends, his ability to study, his overall life. After one Reiki session, he began to understand grounding and how to use it to create a new life for himself. He worked hard daily to maintain his grounding, and during a two year period was able to change his life so drastically that it was unrecognizable from where it was previously. He embraced Reiki as a practice and is now a Reiki Master. He is now stable in his body and is continuing to grow and learn. His living situation has improved as has his relationships with family and friends. He continues to raise his vibration and spiritual connection and is now assisting others on their journeys.

The following is a summary of the Root Chakra:

Sanskrit Name:	Muladhara
Meaning:	Root Support
Location:	Base of Spine, Perineum
Color:	Red
Element:	Earth
Planet:	Mercury
Glands:	Adrenals
Sense:	Smell
Mantra:	LAM
Gemstones:	Ruby, Hematite, Garnet
Issues:	Foundation, Material World, Safety

The following is a daily practice for the first chakra:

1. Chant LAM five long times. Taking a long deep breath in, chant LAM and feel it vibrate to the base of the spine.

2. Stand upon the earth barefoot. Even standing underneath an eave of your house in bad weather or on a wooden floor will help grounding. Visualize the earth as you do this.

3. Wear any type of red clothing.

4. Wear or carry a red stone or crystal.

5. Breathe long and deep many times a day and chant out loud or silently, "I live here, in this body."

Sacral Chakra

The second chakra, or *sacral chakra*, resides halfway between your root chakra and your navel center. It vibrates to the color orange, to the musical note D, and to the chant word VAM (pronounced *VOM*, like *mom*). This chakra is considered your "home base" and is responsible for manifestation, sexuality, creative energy, financial issues, and passion for living. Your ability to manifest whatever it is in your life that you focus on with intention is powered from the sacral chakra. Whether it is creating relationships, children, jobs, money, artistic endeavors; the options are unlimited and depend on an open sacral chakra. This chakra controls the reproductive organs, prostate, bladder, kidneys, and the lower back. If you are having issues with these parts of your body or feel frozen with creative issues, you need to ask yourself if it is time to release old programing that no longer serves you. Working with the second chakra can help you to release, to move forward, to embrace and manifest your dreams.

A client/student with huge issues came to me for a Reiki session. She was stuck, frozen, and unable to move forward with manifestation in her life. We worked extensively on the second chakra. One of the first things she did was to go out and purchase orange undergarments, clothing, crystals, and jewelry. Within weeks her life began to change and move forward. Her daily intentional practice of self Reiki began to open the energetic flow and doors opened quickly. Her work increased as she was self-employed, and her finances stabilized. The life partner she dreamed of entered her life. Creativity flowed from many directions. Joy, sharing, love, stability, all became part of her daily life. After two years, her life was totally different. Today, she is one of the happiest, most loving, optimistic people I know and helps many others through her experience and knowledge.

The following is a summary of the Sacral Chakra:

Sanskrit Name:	Svadhisthana
Meaning:	Sweetness or Loveliness
Location:	Lower Abdomen
Color:	Orange
Element:	Water
Planet:	Venus, Moon
Glands:	Ovaries, Testicles
Sense:	Taste
Mantra:	VAM
Gemstones:	Carnelian, Moonstone, Coral
Issues:	Creativity, Life Energy, Sexuality, Sensuality, Fertility

The following is a daily practice for the second chakra:

1. Chant VAM five long times. Taking a long deep breath in, chant VAM and feel it vibrate deep within the second chakra.

2. Drink lots of water, as this element represents the second chakra.

3. Wear orange. This color vibrates healing energy.

4. Wear or carry an orange stone or crystal.

5. Breathe long and deep many times a day and chant out loud or silently, "I am open to my creative flow".

Solar Plexus Chakra

The third chakra, or *solar plexus chakra*, resides at your navel center. It vibrates to the color yellow, the musical note E, and the chant word RAM (pronounced *ROM*, like *mom*). This chakra represents personal power, being able to stand in self-confidence and self-esteem. This chakra affects all digestion flowing through the stomach, gallbladder, spleen, pancreas, liver, immune system, muscles, and adrenal glands.

From the moment we are born, we are programmed to please everyone around us. This action can actually deplete our personal power as we give to others. As we try to please our parents, family, friends, teachers, bosses, and co-workers, we can become drained. Our societal programming and organized dogma instills patterns of behavior that tend to take away personal power. Does this sound familiar? Follow the rules and someone else's expectations, give beyond your capabilities, and work until you are exhausted and have no time for self-care. It is unfortunate that self-care is often looked upon as being selfish. I have seen many individuals give and give and give until they become totally emotionally, mentally, and physically depleted. At this point, physical symptoms of discomfort and disease can manifest in the organs under the third chakra influence. If you are feeling depleted it is probably time for some self-care. If your car ran out gas you would surely go to the gas station. It is really the same thing. If someone says something demeaning or judgmental and you get the hurt or sick feeling in your stomach, it is time to strengthen your power center, your third chakra. If you have issues with willpower, assertiveness, and self-confidence, these all relate to the solar plexus chakra.

In my previous work caring for interior plants in commercial office buildings, I was exposed to the corporate "non well being" of many employees. As I took care of the plants, many employees engaged me in conversation. The number of people who had gallbladders removed, IBS, stomach issues, emotional burnout, and anxiety, was rampant. Many were on expensive medications. Many asked my advice and I began teaching them how to breathe long and deep five times to relax, how to stretch, and the importance of drinking more water during the day. I encouraged them to set reminders on their computers for these suggestions. I was happy to learn that many individuals began to feel better. Small steps to self-care and empowerment can lead to a huge improvement if practiced daily.

The following is a summary of the Solar Plexus Chakra:

Sanskrit Name:	Manipura
Meaning:	Shining Gem or Place of Gems
Location:	Navel Area
Color:	Yellow
Element:	Fire
Planet:	Mars
Glands:	Pancreas, Adrenals
Sense:	Sight
Mantra:	RAM
Gemstones:	Amber, Topaz, Yellow Citrine
Issues:	Willpower, Assertiveness, Self-confidence

The following is a daily practice for the third chakra:

1. Chant RAM five long times. Taking a long deep breath in, chant RAM and feel it vibrate in the abdomen, navel center.

2. Stand up for yourself, your beliefs, kindly yet firmly. Set boundaries.

2. Wear any shade of yellow somewhere on your body.

3. Wear or carry a yellow stone or crystal.

5. Breathe long and deep many times a day and chant out loud or silently, "I am strong."

Heart Chakra

The fourth chakra, or *heart chakra*, resides in your heart center. It vibrates to the colors green and pink, the musical note F, and to the chant word YAM (pronounced *YOM*, like *mom*). This chakra connects the three lower and three upper chakras through the heart. The heart chakra represents pure compassion and unconditional love. Your emotions live here. Our spiritual awakening and connection begin in this chakra. All healing stems from this chakra. The fourth chakra also includes the lungs, representing our ability to breathe in our *Prana*, our life force.

The heart is the first organ to develop in the womb. It vibrates at a higher rate than any other organ and relates to all of the other organs with every beat. The heart is the master organ. We can be brain-dead and still be alive, but once the heart stops, all other organs cease as well.

When you have extreme stress or anxiety, tightening of your chest, shallow breathing, all of this is found in your fourth chakra. Fear, stress, grief, anger, inability to move, all trigger anxiety which is related to the heart chakra. Self-love, forgiveness, and self respect are all associated with this chakra. All are important to your personal healing and growth.

Over my years of teaching and doing thousands of private Reiki sessions, I have observed that a majority of clients experience little to no self-love. Programming and traumas have squelched their ability to embrace their own value. Healing begins and ends here, in the heart chakra.

There is a simple mantra taught at the beginning of one of my classes: "Bountiful am I, Blissful am I, Beautiful am I." Few students can chant this right away. Many cry, many cannot let these words pass their lips. For many it takes months to even be able to whisper these words, to embrace them. Our society has not nurtured or taught self-love and respect. Your spirit loves you more than anyone else will ever love you. It has chosen to live in your current vehicle, your body. Recognizing and tuning in to your spirit, allowing the love to flow through every cell of your body, is the beginning of true honor and love.

Finding the root of discomfort will eventually go through all of the other chakras and end up in the heart. Traumas of betrayal, abuse, abandonment, etc., from this life and past lives, come back to our ability to love, forgive, and release. All of these energies require compassion from the heart to heal. There are studies that show finding the vibration of your heart will allow the healing of traumas, cancers, and other health issues in your body, mind, emotions, and spirit. Gregg Braden, New York Times best-selling Hay House author, has several amazing YouTube videos on addressing this theory: *www.greggbraden.com*

The following is a summary of the Heart Chakra:

Sanskrit Name:	Anahata
Meaning:	Whole, Unstuck
Location:	Center of Chest at Heart Level
Color:	Green, Pink
Element:	Air
Planet:	Jupiter
Glands:	Thymus
Sense:	Touch
Mantra:	YAM
Gemstones:	Emerald, Rose Quartz
Issues:	Love, Compassion

The following is a daily practice for the fourth chakra.

1. Chant YAM five long times. Taking a long deep breath in, chant YAM feel it vibrate in the heart chakra. Do this many times during the day.

2. Practice true forgiveness for yourself and others.

3. Wear green or pink clothing.

4. Wear or carry green or pink stones or crystals.

5. Breathe long and deep many times a day and chant a variety of mantras out loud or silently: "I love myself;" "I am worthy;" "I believe it in every cell of my body."

Throat Chakra

The fifth chakra, or *throat chakra*, resides in the throat. It vibrates to the color light blue, to the musical note G, and the chant word HAM (pronounced *HOM*, like *mom*). This chakra represents your ability to speak your truth and communicate with others. It connects the heart chakra and the third eye chakra, balancing thoughts and feelings. This chakra affects your thyroid, thymus, upper vertebrae, and tongue.

Hundreds of people and clients that I have met and worked with have thyroid issues and poor communication skills. Many people have been and are being raised with the idea that they are not allowed to talk or to speak. "Shut up," "You don't know what you're talking about," and "Children should be seen and not heard," these sayings are all too common in our society today. It also seems that speaking and talking is taking a back seat to "texting" in today's world. To open your throat chakra, you must find your voice and speak your truth.

A 60-year old professional, who was excellent at his job, came to see me for a Reiki session. As we spoke, he could not complete a sentence. His mind was scattered and he was unable to follow and complete a thought. The words he spoke did not fit together coherently. After a brief discussion about the chakras, he was ready for his Reiki session.

As my hands flowed slightly above his body and passed by his throat, he felt the energy and began coughing. I asked him, "What does it feel like?" His gasping answer was "a gag." Leaning over him on the Reiki table, I suggested that he pull the gag out, empowering him to do so. For the next 10 minutes I watched him pull out the energetic gag. I felt that he had been gagged all of this lifetime and perhaps beyond. He was exhausted after the energetic ordeal. The Reiki energy flowed in after the pulling, filling the void of all of the energy that had been released with loving Reiki energy. His energy returned and he said he felt lighter, happier, and was able to talk in slow, complete sentences. He was done swallowing his words.

It is important to speak from your heart. Take a deep breath and begin every sentence, whether aloud or silently, "My truth is," or "I feel," or "I believe." Speak with intention and open the flow of your voice.

The following is a summary of the Throat Chakra:

Sanskrit Name: Vishuddha
Meaning: Pure
Location: Throat

Color:	Light Blue
Element:	Ether
Planet:	Mercury
Glands:	Thyroid, Parathyroid
Sense:	Hearing
Mantra:	HAM
Gemstones:	Turquoise, Aquamarine
Issues:	Communication, Creativity, Truthfulness

The following is a daily practice for the fifth chakra:

1. Chant HAM five long times. Taking a long deep breath in, chant HAM and feel it vibrate in your throat, thyroid, and thymus. Continue to do so as needed during the day.

2. Begin each sentence silently or aloud with "My truth is," "I believe," or "I feel," as you communicate with others.

3. Wear light blue clothing.

4. Wear or carry light blue stones or crystals.

5. Chant or sing silently many times a day: "I honor my voice," "I honor my truth," or "I am safe to communicate."

Third Eye Chakra

The sixth chakra, or *third eye chakra*, resides in the middle of your forehead slightly above your eyebrows. Vibrating to the color indigo, the musical note A, and the chant word OM, this chakra can be awakened. It represents intuition and wisdom, and is referred to as your spirit voice/mind. You know immediately when you hear something if it is true or false for you. This chakra allows you to see clearly. This is the wisdom of the third eye.

When you listen to the initial "yes or no," " true or false," that you receive upon hearing something, you need to ask yourself, "Do I have the strength to stand in my truth?" If you ask a question and hear the answer, do you go into debate of what others want you to think, or do you follow your own answer, the intuition you have received? If you choose another path, other than your initial answer, get ready to take a little side journey, a lesson needing to be learned. If you have a sense of knowing, understanding, or seeing that which has never been explained, this is your third eye in action. Intuition is a real ability and gift, a talent. Now is the time to open and strengthen it to greater capacity.

At times, programmed knowledge does not serve your highest personal good. Your spirit knows what is best for you on your current journey. Listen to and follow this guidance. Perhaps you had imaginary friends when young or felt the presence of others in your space. Awareness, intuition and a higher sense of consciousness and vibration have not been taught or recognized by our current societies for ages. NOW is the time to WAKE UP! Develop, trust, and move forward with confidence to your inner knowledge that connects you to unlimited information and guidance.

The following is a summary of the Third Eye Chakra:

Sanskrit Name:	Ajna
Meaning:	To Know, To Perceive
Location:	Center of Forehead
Color:	Indigo
Element:	Light
Planet:	Uranus
Glands:	Pineal
Sense:	None
Mantra:	OM
Gemstones:	Blue Sapphire, Opal
Issues:	Intuition, Wisdom, Knowing

The following is a daily practice for the sixth chakra:

1. Chant OM many, many times a day.

2. Listen to your first answer/guidance and upon hearing it, stand true in your power.

3. Wear indigo,white, and blue clothing.

4. Place an indigo crystal/stone on your third eye when at rest. Keep them in your pocket and wear them on your body.

5. Meditate with intention and ask to be more open to seeing clearly.

Crown Chakra

The seventh chakra, or *crown chakra*, resides at the top of your head. It vibrates to the color violet to white, the musical note B, and there is no chant word. This chakra directly connects your spirit to highest consciousness, divine wisdom, great Creator, God/Goddess energy, whatever is your word that describes your belief in a higher consciousness. Visualizing the opening of your crown and connecting to your highest source is the key to the seventh chakra.

This chakra can assist you in raising your vibration and spiritual consciousness beyond your dreams. Being open and trusting, using the phrase *highest light guidance* before any other words, connects you to the pure, compassionate, unconditional infinite love. While Reiki and working with the chakras is not a religion, this connection can strengthen any religious belief you may have. Spirituality is personal. Everyone has direct accessibility to this energetic source.

Oneness, not separation, is the flow of energy here. Being connected to everything in existence becomes part of your reality. Become a calming and uniting being at home and at work. Honor everyone and everything around you. Everyone is doing the best they can with the knowledge they possess. There is no judgement. Allow everyone their journey.

Daily intentional practice opens this chakra to receiving more cosmic input and raises your personal vibration. This allows you to see with fresh eyes, to rise above the heaviness of the collective consciousness, and start living your life to your fullest potential.

The following is a summary of the Crown Chakra:

Sanskrit Name:	Sahasrara
Meaning:	Thousandfold
Location:	Top of Head
Color:	Violet
Element:	Thought
Planet:	Neptune
Glands:	Pituitary
Sense:	Cosmic Awareness
Mantra:	Silent
Gemstones:	Diamond, Amethyst
Issues:	Enlightenment, Spirituality, Cosmic Consciousness

The follow is a daily practice for the seventh chakra:

1. Connect the energy from your heart chakra to and through your crown to your highest consciousness.

2. Be kind to everything.

3. Wear violet/white clothing.

4. Wear or carry violet/white stones or crystals.

5. Meditate with the intention of opening your crown and connecting to your "Highest Light Guidance."

Earth Chakra

The Earth Chakra is located approximately two to four feet beneath the feet. The purpose of the Earth Chakra is grounding. As Cyndi Dale mentions in her book, *New Chakra Healing: The Revolutionary 32-Center Energy System* (1998), "To be grounded means that we are fully attached to the earth; we are "in" our bodies. Grounded people can draw on their full faculties, abilities, and experiences, and thus, are able to handle any situation. In this way, they are comparable to the Shambhallic warrior who lives fully fearless and ready for action" (54). As would be expected, the colors of the Earth Chakra are earth tones, including browns, greens, and yellows. This chakra contains the four earth elements: fire, earth, water, and air.

Star Chakra

The Star Chakra is located approximately two inches above the head. It is believed that this chakra is the portal out of our time/space continuum. The Akashic records are also thought to be accessible through this chakra. Cyndi Dale states, "Here one also finds the Akashic records, the books upon which is recorded all we have ever seen, done, or said, in this life or any other. Because of this, we can gain access to anything about our past through the eight chakra. If appropriate, we can read the pasts of others. We can journey to any place that exists in the present or in other dimensions and probe into potential or destined futures. It is also possible to read alternative pasts, presents, and futures here" (48). The color is silver or ultraviolet. The chakra is associated with visual images such as the moon, stars, other dimensions, and time itself.

CHAKRA BALANCING MEDITATION

Sit comfortably with your spine as straight as possible, your feet flat on the floor or legs in easy pose.

Place your hands in Gassho, thumbs touching your heart.

Close your eyes. Take a few long slow deep breaths and slowly exhale out any tension or tightness. Relax the muscles around your ribs and any other area that may be constricting a full breath.

In your mind's eye, visualize and connect with the Earth Star, beneath your feet.

Feel your crown opening, connecting through your Crown and Star chakras to your highest mind, Cosmos, Divine infinite connection, brightest light from Source.

Slowly, starting from the Earth chakra, bring your long deep breath from the Earth through your entire body, to your light connection. Repeat three to five times.

When you feel relaxed, on your next breath up, chant LAM. Relax your chin. Open your mouth, do not clench your lips or teeth. Feel this long note vibrate your Root chakra for the entire breath. Repeat at least three times. Continue until you feel your Root chakra vibrating.

Once your Root chakra is vibrating, move up to your Sacral chakra.
Keep your chin relaxed and your spine straight. Feel the Earth chakra beneath your feet and your Crown and Star chakra opening to even greater amounts of Divine light flowing from the Cosmos.
Long deep breath, chant VAM. Feel your Sacral chakra vibrating with the long exhalation.
Repeat at least three times. Continue until you feel your Sacral chakra vibrating.
Now feel your Root and Sacral chakras vibrating together with the next breath.
Repeat this breath at least three times. Continue until you feel them spinning together.

Once you feel these two chakras spinning together, move up to your Solar Plexus chakra.
Keep your chin relaxed and your spine straight. Feel the Earth chakra beneath your feet and your Crown and Star chakra opening to even greater amounts of Divine light flowing from the Cosmos.
Long deep breath, chant RAM. Feel your Solar Plexus chakra vibrating with the long exhalation.
Repeat this breath at least three times. Continue until you feel your Solar Plexus chakra vibrating.
Now feel your Root, Sacral and Solar Plexus chakras vibrating together with the next breath.
Repeat this breath at least three times. Continue until you feel them spinning together.

Once you feel these three chakras spinning together, move up to your Heart chakra.
Keep your chin relaxed and your spine straight. Feel the Earth chakra beneath your feet and your Crown and Star chakra opening to even greater amounts of Divine light flowing from the Cosmos.
Long deep breath, chant YAM. Feel your Heart chakra vibrating with the long exhalation.

Repeat at least three times. Continue until you feel your Heart chakra vibrating. Feel the Heart growing, expanding with greater volumes of sound moving up from your lower chakras and more light flowing down from the Cosmos. Visualize your Heart as a glowing, growing, radiant expanding star.
Now feel your Root, Sacral, Solar Plexus, and Heart chakras vibrating together with the next breath. Repeat this breath at least three times. Continue until you feel them spinning together.

Once you feel these four chakras spinning together, move up to your Throat chakra.
Keep your chin relaxed and your spine straight. Feel the Earth chakra beneath your feet and your Crown and Star chakra opening to even greater amounts of Divine light flowing from the Cosmos.
Long deep breath, chant HAM. Feel your Throat chakra vibrating with the long exhalation. Feel the physical throat opening and expanding, allowing a greater volume of sound to vibrate through.
Repeat at least three times. Continue until you feel your Throat chakra fully open and vibrating.
Now feel your Root, Sacral, Solar Plexus, Heart, and Throat chakras vibrating together with the next longer, deeper breath. Repeat this breath at least three times. Continue until you feel them spinning together.

Once you feel these five chakras spinning together, move up to your Third Eye chakra.
Keep your chin relaxed and your spine straight. Feel the Earth chakra beneath your feet and your Crown and Star chakra opening to even greater amounts of Divine light flowing from the Cosmos.
Long deep breath, chant OM. Feel your Third Eye chakra vibrating with the long exhalation. Feel the pineal and pituitary glands, behind your Third Eye, opening and expanding, allowing a greater volume of light and sound to vibrate through. Repeat at least three times. Continue until you feel your Third Eye chakra fully open and vibrating. Now feel your Root, Sacral, Solar Plexus, Heart, Throat, and Third Eye chakras vibrating together with the next longer, deeper breath. Repeat this breath at least three times. Continue until you feel them spinning together.

Once you feel these six chakras spinning together, move up to your Crown chakra.
Keep your chin relaxed and your spine straight. Feel the Earth chakra beneath your feet and your Crown and Star chakra opening to even greater amounts of Divine light flowing from the Cosmos.
Long deep breath, slowly exhale. Feel your Crown chakra vibrating and opening to even greater volumes of cosmic light flowing, with the long exhalation. Feel the pineal and pituitary glands, behind your Third Eye, opening and expanding more, allowing a greater volume of light to flow through.
Repeat at least three times. Continue until you feel your Crown chakra fully open and vibrating.
Now feel your Root, Sacral, Solar Plexus, Heart, Throat, Third Eye, and Crown chakras vibrating and flowing together with the next longer, deeper breath. Repeat this breath at least three times. Continue until you feel them spinning together.

With your seven chakras spinning together, connected to your Earth and Star chakras, feel the movement and opening of your central channel. You now have a direct connection to infinite, Divine Light from Source and a grounding with the Mother Earth. You may experience a feeling of pure joy, euphoria, see colors, feel or see your Light Guides, or have many other amazing experiences.

Relax with your hands on your thighs, palms facing up in the receiving gesture, mudra.

Being connected and in balance is an opportune time to enjoy being completely relaxed, ask for guidance, release emotions or trauma, journey, etc, or just "BE."

SPINNING CHAKRAS

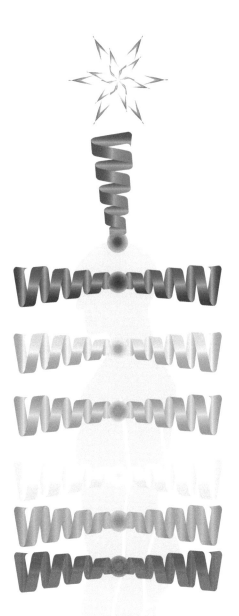

AURIC FIELD LAYERS

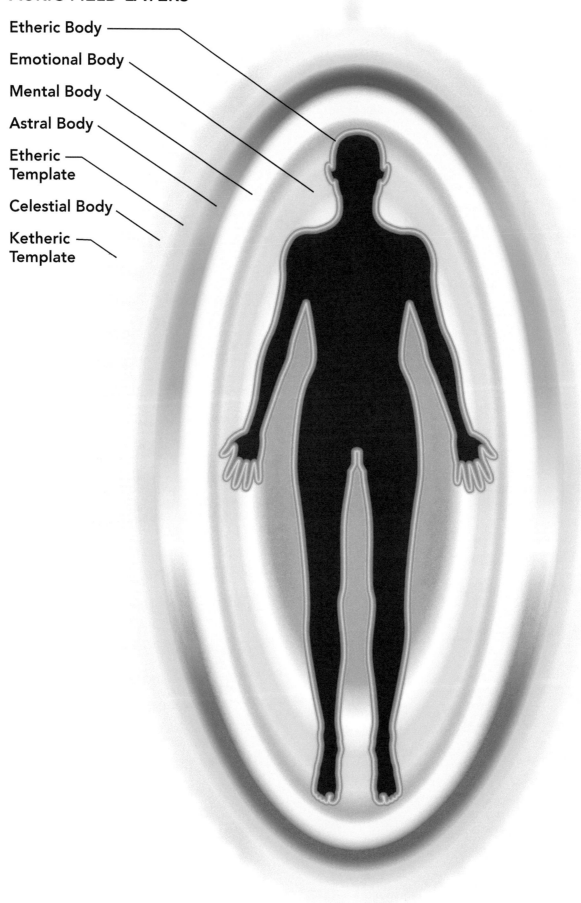

Etheric Body

Emotional Body

Mental Body

Astral Body

Etheric Template

Celestial Body

Ketheric Template

AURIC FIELD

The auric field is important to discuss since it is an interconnected field of energetic layers or *subtle bodies* around the physical body. These layers are connected to the body via energy points commonly known as *chakras*.

The auric field is known as a holographic energetic template, or the biomagnetic field that surrounds our physical body. This field can be detected and seen by psychics, some energetic healers, and photographed with Kirlian photography.

Cyndi Dale, in her book *New Chakra Healing: The Revolutionary 32-Center Energy System* (1998), explains the connection between the chakra system and the auric field: "Many psychics differentiate the esoteric bodies this way: the aura is on the outside of the body; the chakras are on the inside. Though this theory can conceptually help us, it does not tell the entire story. Nature doesn't really differentiate between the insides and outsides of things. The truth is, the chakras are holistic units that tie into, interact with, and help form the auric layers. These auric layers are also holistic units. The aura as a whole includes the chakras and every other aspect of our being. It is also a sub-unit of our energetic self because its major functions enable us to interact with our external environment and the physical, mental, emotional, and spiritual dimensions that are constantly at play with our being" (134).

The auric field is your first line of defense and protection. It is a highly effective shield against external forces. Because it is not well known, especially in the western world, it has not received care. Just as we must daily care for all parts of our body, we must also daily take care of our auric field. The auric field can expand up to nine feet when healthy. It is composed of seven subtle, energetic, multidimensional layers. Each layer increases in higher vibration as it moves away from the Physical body. It appears as an elongated sphere of light encompassing our entire physical form. Each layer can carry and reflect the colors of the in-body chakras and more. As the vibration grows, so does the shimmering glow of the colors.

The first level of the auric field is the Etheric body.

This body overlays the Physical body, expanding directly from it to about one and a half inches beyond the physical form. It carries information which guides cellular growth to the developing fetus, throughout the lifespan, and to the healthy, damaged, or diseased adult body. The Physical body cannot exist without the Etheric body. When the Etheric body is damaged or traumatized, it creates physical *disease*. The Physical and Etheric bodies totally relate and speak to each other. A bluish glow is detected by Kirlian photography in this layer.

The second level of the auric field is the Emotional body.

This layer extends one to three inches beyond the Physical body. This layer is the seat of human emotions, where the "feelings" live. Emotional trauma held in this layer can cause a disruption in the vibrational rhythm of the layer, creating an imbalance to be picked up by the Etheric and transmitted to the Physical. A domino effect can be created, just as in the chakras. A rainbow of colors can be detected in this layer.

The third level of the auric field is the Mental body.

This layer extends three to eight inches beyond the Physical body. This layer holds our ideas and mental processes. Our ability to organize, disseminate information, grow beyond old programming, broaden our scope of understanding and possibilities, all reside here. The energies of being inflexible and stuck in old paradigms will flow through the Emotional and Etheric bodies to the Physical body and can create dis-ease. Yellow light can be detected in this field.

The fourth level of the auric field is the Astral body.

This layer extends about one foot beyond the Physical body. It is the bridge and doorway to spiritual connection. The Astral body is a containment vehicle for the personality beyond physical death. There is a strong association with the heart chakra. All colors may be detected here. This is where near death experiences can happen. It is also the field that psychics tap into for readings.

The fifth level of the auric field is the Etheric template.

This layer extends one to two feet beyond the Physical body. Deep blues can be detected in this layer. It is the blueprint of the physical world in another, higher vibrational dimension. The Etheric template is related to the throat chakra. Sound creates matter. Sound healing is most effective in this layer of the Auric field. The Etheric blueprint directly speaks to the Etheric body for physical, mental, emotional wellness and balance.

The sixth level of the auric field is the Celestial body.

It is associated with enlightenment and the third eye. This layer extends two to three feet beyond the Physical body. It opens access to higher knowledge and spiritual consciousness. Shimmery, pastel colors can be found in this layer. The Celestial body connects us to our purpose in life and to unconditional love. It vibrates at an extremely high level.

The seventh level of the auric field is the Ketheric template, the Causal body.

Divine and universal consciousness represent this level. This level reflects all experiences in current and previous lives. Oneness with all, connection with the Divine, is the energy present here. The Ketheric template connects directly to the crown chakra. It holds all the other layers of the auric field together. Golden rays of light flow through this layer of the auric field. These vibrations are the highest light vibration that one can experience in physical form.

Rosalyn L. Bruyere in her book, *Wheels of Light: Chakras, Auras, and the Healing Energy of the Body* (1994), summarizes the auric field: "The auric field is a metaphor for life. In other words, a person's energy field or the individual aura around the body, which is created and controlled by the chakras, reflects how one's life actually live; it mirrors the flow of that life. In this way, the auric field becomes more than a symbol for life. The aura is life" (61).

AURA STRENGTHENING EXERCISE

This exercise, when practiced with intention, fills the holes and weak areas in your auric field. The auric field is the first line of energetic defense and protection.

Stand with your feet hip width apart and your hands resting at your sides, palms facing outward.

Feel the earth beneath your feet.

Raise your arms slowly, bringing the Earth energy up through all the layers of your auric field.

Once you arrive above the top of your head, clap your hands.

The clapping changes the vibration of what is around and within you.
(Like when a baby shakes a rattle and begins to laugh instead of cry).

Slowly move your hands apart approximately two feet, palms still facing each other. In this position, you are receiving immense cosmic energy.

Without stopping the flowing movement, turn your hands away from each other and slowly bring them down through all the layers of your auric field, filling them with the cosmic energy.

As you reach the sides of your legs, slap the side of your thighs grounding this cosmic energy into your body through your feet and into the earth.

Repeat this movement many times. The more repetitions, the stronger your auric field becomes.

This movement can be done as slowly or as quickly as you desire.

Performing this movement first thing in the morning strengthens your auric field for the day.

This movement can be repeated many times a day, whenever you feel you need more strength or protection, for whatever reason.

It takes 40 days to establish a new pattern of behavior. This movement will become part of your daily practice and keep you strong and protected as you start and move through your day.

REIKI
WHAT IT IS AND HOW IT WORKS

Reiki is a word composed of two Japanese words, *Rei* and *Ki*. Rei is commonly interpreted to mean higher knowledge, higher wisdom. Ki is commonly interpreted to mean life force, life energy. The definition I use for Reiki is *Spiritually Guided Life Force Energy*.

Reiki is a form of vibrational healing. In his book, *Vibrational Medicine: The #1 Handbook Of Subtle-Energy Therapies* (2001), Richard Gerber states "...we, as human organisms are a series of interacting multidimensional subtle-energy systems, and that if these energy systems become imbalanced there may be resulting pathological symptoms which manifest on the physical/emotional/mental/spiritual planes. These imbalances can be healed by rebalancing the subtle energy templates with the right frequency of vibrational medicine" (18). Each organ vibrates to its own specific vibration.

William Lee Rand, in his book *Reiki For A New Millennium* (1998), discusses Reiki: "Reiki is a Japanese technique for stress reduction and relaxation that also promotes healing. It uses no technology at all and is an effective method of gaining balance in our modern lives. It can help alleviate many of the problems our transforming society is creating and also stimulate feelings of love, peace, harmony, joy and all the other qualities needed in the new millennium. Based on subtle life energy that flows through one's hands, a Reiki treatment produces a warm glowing radiance that nurtures and restores vitality. Reiki can be self-administered as well as used to treat others. One of the most amazing things about Reiki is that it can be sent at a distance to help others or directed to global crises" (v).

Reiki enhances other healing methods. It amplifies by raising the vibration of whatever other healing method is being used. Reiki does not take the place of modern medicine, but can work hand in hand for one's overall healing experience. The flowing, compassionate energy of Reiki can enhance a patient's ability to bring their mental and emotional bodies into balance so the physical can begin to heal. Holding and infusing medications with Reiki before taking them can enhance their effectiveness.

Whether the recipient believes in the energy or not, it will work to their highest good on some level. It does not matter what religion or ideology they have. The vibrational light energy does not interfere with any belief system. Reiki cannot be forced. Even an unconscious person's spirit will make the choice to receive it or not. Reiki energy works on everything, all species.

Animals and plants love Reiki energy and most accept willingly, even from a great distance. When Reiki is sent to other parts of the world and universe, it always flows for the highest good to whoever or whatever needs or accepts the energy. It revitalizes life force energy in all things. Reiki helps to locate the source or root of dis-ease and begins the healing process. This energy is absorbed by the body, mind, emotions, or spirit of whatever or whoever it is intentionally being sent or given to.

Reiki can be used to cleanse and bless any being, object, dwelling, workspace, or physical location such as the oceans, the mountains, the forests, etc.

Reiki can be used to purify and heal karma by continual clearing, cleansing, forgiving, and blessing with the light energy daily. It crosses all time, the time wave of past, present, and future. Time is all one continuous flow. Reiki, sent with intention to all time at once, enhances and speeds up one's overall healing process. There is a belief that as one heals, they heal for the past seven generations, current, and future generations. Reiki is infinite, unconditional love, highest light vibration from Divine source, that exists everywhere.

The first thing someone does when they hurt, or their pet hurts, is to place their hands on the area of discomfort and pour healing love through their hands. Reiki does this and more. Because it is spiritually guided healing energy, directly from Divine source, it is more powerful. The Reiki practitioner connects to the infinite source of energy by plugging directly into Divine source. The energy flows from Divine source through the practitioner's crown, heart, then hands into the recipient's body.

This Divine energy has its own intelligence and knows where to go in the body of the recipient. Through intention of healing for the highest good of the recipient's physical, emotional, mental, or spiritual body, the Divine connection provides the flow of the energetic healing. The Reiki practitioner is the physical tool through which this healing energy flows. There is no will or ego attached to the outcome, as the practitioner does not know what the highest good of the recipient is. The Reiki practitioner is there to provide whatever comfort or healing is needed by the recipient on their personal journey in this lifetime. Only the Spirit, Soul of the recipient has this knowledge. Sometimes a person will not physically heal. This is their choice, their spirit's choice. It is possible that there is lesson for them to learn in this lifetime by experiencing their dis-ease. If they can embrace peace with their journey, that is what the Reiki energy will bring them. Reiki is a compassionate, spiritual practice and a vibrational tool for energetic healing.

When I was still taking care of plants in commercial offices, many employees started asking me to place my hands on their necks, shoulders, or head, to alleviate their pain and discomfort at their desks. I had them close their eyes, breathe, and relax as the Reiki energy flowed through my hands to their area of discomfort. After five minutes, their pain subsided and they were able to continue working.

A client came for a Reiki session after a motorcycle accident. Her left eye, still drooping almost shut, had not recovered from the injury. Never having experienced Reiki before, she was totally open to anything that could possibly heal her eye. After getting her comfortable on the Reiki table, I proceeded to run Reiki energy through her auric field and chakras. Cutting away and dissolving energetic shadows, attachments, and fear concerning the accident, I then began to flow Reiki to her neck and eyes. When the session was complete, I helped her to sit up and handed her a mirror. Her eye was healed and her beautiful face was radiant once again!

Strangers have called me for a Reiki session to calm their fears before surgery. They would come for a session a day or two before surgery, receive Reiki to calm their fears, and leave with calming breath exercises. I would then be at the hospital, pre-surgery, continue to give them Reiki, and roll them into the procedure. Afterwards, as they were in recovery, Reiki was again given. They were joyous and calm as they recovered, many in a quicker than normal recovery time. There are medical studies which show that Reiki can bring calmness, lower blood pressure, and increase healing, before and after surgical procedures.

Reiki can be used in a variety of ways, none of which can cause any harm. I teach a Reiki method which places protective Reiki energy over people, places, and things. I refer to this as a dome of protective light.

A highly educated, left-brain professional psychologist came to me to learn Reiki. She needed Reiki for psychic protection at work and for overall protection in her life. She lived alone in a nice but older, mixed energy area of town. There was an alley on the side on the apartment complex where she lived. As the days became shorter, she began arriving home from work after dark. The alley was being used as a bathroom by the homeless people in the area.

Remembering the technique, she went across the street and began placing a dome of protective light and love over her building. As she was doing this, a homeless person walked in front of her building and paused to pick up cigarette butts out of a container. As the person bent over, it appeared as if she was repelled, unable to continue her action. She bent over again and the same thing happened. With a startled look on her face, she hurried on and left the area.

My student immediately called me and recounted the story. She was totally astonished and amazed at what she had just witnessed. As the days went on, my student maintained the dome of protection over her building and the alley. Over time, the street people stopped using the alley and the area became a safer place to live.

Another Reiki student had been harassed and bullied at work by a co-worker for some time. She felt she might have to leave her employer and find another job. The day after her Reiki training, she arrived at her cubicle workstation early. She activated the Reiki energy of love and light and asked that no harm or aggressive energy enter her cubicle.

During the first day, the bully could not enter her cubicle but stood at the opening and made negative verbal comments. On day two, the student again activated the Reiki around her workspace. The bully did not even stand in the doorway but peered over the cubicle way. By the end of the week, all harassment had stopped and the bully could not even walk down her hallway. The student felt safe, more relaxed, and was able to continue her employment.

Arriving home from work one day, I was met by my neighbors who were very upset and angry. Across our street is a small park bordering a lake. There was a couple with two small children at the park. The parents were allowing the toddler to chase a duck who had a broken wing.

My neighbors could not get the city's animal control department to respond. They pleaded with me to do something. I walked to the front of my house and observed the poor duck being chased. I sent a dome of Reiki light energy over the duck for its protection. I also sent light, love, and healing Reiki energy for the highest good of everyone in the park. Within minutes, the family packed up their things and left the park. The duck was able to make it back to the lake and to safety.

I have found that Reiki can be a calming energy in other situations as well. On several occasions while waiting for a flight at an airport, I have witnessed unhappy children, usually crying or fussing. Using my Reiki which I always keep activated, I have sent light, love, and Reiki energy to the child and parent. In most cases the child has looked at me directly, calmed down, and become peaceful. Reiki is a compassionate, peaceful energy.

Reiki is an evolving practice. I believe that practitioners will be guided and given enhanced tools and techniques when the situation warrants. I also believe that healers can have assistance from other realms when it is needed.

I received a phone call early one morning from a Reiki Master who was also a student of mine. She could barely speak. Her youngest daughter, who had just turned 21, was in the hospital in critical condition. When I arrived at the hospital, the mother was in shock, sitting beside her daughter. The young girl was hooked up to multiple lifesaving machines.

This is how the young woman ended up in the hospital: To celebrate her 21st birthday, the daughter went to Germany. This had been her dream. She was fluent in German and infatuated with the history of WWII. While in Germany, she visited many of the concentration camps and memorials.

Her elation from the trip was short-lived after she returned home. She became very depressed and had a difficult time coping with life. Her volatile relationship with her stepfather got worse and he criticized her every action. Her self-esteem was at an all time low.

The daughter lived in a basement apartment with a young couple upstairs. They noticed her depression and decided to help her feel better. One of them, a heroin addict, came down and assisted by injecting a powerful dose of heroin into the young woman. She was found on the floor, unconscious, by a good friend who had come by to check on her. The friend called for medical attention and the young woman was taken to the hospital.

When the mother arrived at the hospital, she was told by the doctor that her daughter was not expected to live, given her current condition. According the physician, she was brain-dead and her organs were failing. She was at the point of no return.

The mother was not allowed to enter the daughter's room, given her grave condition. All the mother could do was lean against the outside wall and send Reiki to her daughter. As the nurse was cleaning the barely-alive body of the daughter, the young woman opened her eyes. The nurse, shocked by this, immediately called for the doctor.

From that moment on, the young woman was known around the hospital as the "miracle patient." The hospital staff hooked the daughter up to life support systems and allowed the mother into the room. Since the heroin dose was so strong and the patient had never used the drug, the doctors held little hope for recovery. The medical staff was not spirituality orientated and was not inclined to believe in miracles.

When I arrived at the hospital room, I immediately went to the mother, held her, and gave her the healing light and love of Reiki. The hardest thing that a parent can hear is that no one knows the highest good of the spirit of their child. We do not know the person's journey. I told the mother that all we could do is to send Reiki for the child's highest good.

I stood at the end of the bed, holding the Reiki energy and saying a prayer. I asked that this young woman's spirit be able to have a choice about living or dying, and for her highest light guides and guardians to come to assist the spirit in making the choice.

As I held the energy, Jesus appeared by the daughter's right shoulder and Mother Mary appeared by her left shoulder. The light in the room intensified and became very bright. I held the Reiki energy for the next hour and observed both Jesus and Mother Mary pulling long black threads from the girl's body. As they pulled the threads, they offered them up to the light.

It was during this time that I was given an advanced Reiki healing technique. This technique is taught in the Reiki Level 2 class. The technique was to mentally weave a mesh or net of Reiki symbols around the young women's organs. This was needed to stop the internal bleeding and to assist in a quicker recovery.

After about an hour, the Ascended Masters faded into a bright light. The room was then filled with angels. I told the mother what I had seen, and with tears flowing, she said she could feel and begin to see the angelic forms also. I left the room filled and sealed with healing Reiki energy.

Returning the next morning, I discovered more miracles. The brain-dead daughter was now answering questions by blinking her eyes and squeezing her hands. Family members began coming from other states. The young women began improving daily and the life support equipment was slowly being removed. It seemed that miracles were happening daily.

After eight days, the young women walked out of the hospital having logical thoughts, full speaking capacity, and good coordination. The only memory loss was the night of the trauma. The young woman returned to school and found a good job. She has had only short-term memory issues.

It was after teaching the weaving technique in one of my classes that I was given an epiphany. I remembered that I had observed Jesus and Mary pulling thousands of black threads from the young woman's body. The black threads were the shattered energies of many individuals who had perished in the concentration camps, the fractures of their spirits left behind. The daughter picked up the attachments and absorbed them into her energetic body and brought them home with her. It is no wonder that her depression was so deep.

As the Ascended Masters removed each thread and sent it to the light, the threads were reconnected with the spirits of those who had suffered and perished in the camps. The daughter was the vehicle for that reunion. Here, spirit chose and survived the journey. She was able to assist in the healing of those individuals in a most wonderful and miraculous way.

Over the last 16 years of practicing and teaching Reiki, new methods and techniques have been given to me by highest light guides, guardians, angels, archangels, and Ascended Masters. One technique is to visualize Reiki light energy running through your veins to melt away blockages and to increase circulation. Another technique is to visualize planting a star of Reiki light energy in an organ to melt away obstructions such as gallstones and kidney stones. Both of these techniques have been effective in many cases and the clients have been able to avoid surgery. Both of these techniques are taught in the Maha Reiki® Level 2 class.

The discussion of Reiki would be incomplete without an understanding of how Reiki is passed from Reiki Master Teacher to student. Through the act of receiving an attunement, initiation, or empowerment from a Reiki Master Teacher, one's ability to channel infinite Reiki healing energy from Divine source is opened. This energy flows through the Teacher's connection to Divine source, their heart, hands, and into the student's energetic body.

The flow of light healing energy reboots the energetic fields of the student, raising their vibration. The student's energetic system, residing within and around their body, gets re-wired, upgraded to operate at a higher vibration. As one raises their vibration, they are able to reach higher levels of consciousness.

At the time of attunement, the student also receives a Reiki guide, a higher vibrational light being, that assists in the Reiki practice. Depending on the Reiki Master Teacher, there are usually three or four levels including the Master level. As with any energetic healing work, the more it is used the stronger it becomes. I have seen instances where a Reiki Level 1 practitioner who uses their Reiki daily is much more powerful than a Reiki Master who lets the energy lie dormant.

SUMMARY

- *Reiki* is a Japanese word
- *Rei* means higher knowledge, wisdom
- *Ki* means life force energy
- Reiki means *Spiritually Guided Life Force Energy*
- Reiki is a form of compassionate vibrational healing and enhances all other healing methods

Reiki...

- Works for the highest good and is not considered a religion
- Does not interfere with any religious belief system
- Energy has its own healing intelligence
- Can assist in calming fears
- Cannot be forced
- Cannot cause harm
- Can be used as protective energy
- Can amplify blessings and prayers
- Can be used on plants, animals, people, mother earth, and the cosmos
- Can be used to cleanse any object
- Can be used over long distances
- Can be used to heal karma
- Can be used for healing the past, present, or the future
- Is an evolving healing practice

Francene Hart

MEDITATION FOR ATTUNEMENT

Sit comfortably with your back straight, feet touching the floor, and your hands, palms touching, placed at your heart chakra.

Relax the muscles around your rib cage. Feel the Earth beneath your feet.

Imagine your breath coming up from the Earth, through your feet, ankles, knees, hips, and up through all of your chakras.

As you slowly exhale, release any tension or tightness the breath has found along the way.

Continue this breath, opening and connecting all of your chakras.

Once you feel the smooth flow of breath and energy, melt into deeper relaxation. No worries, only your energy flowing and the balance of this moment is with you.

Continue to experience this flow……..

On your next breath, as you exhale, allow your crown chakra to open to even greater capacity, to receive highest light energy from your Divine Source connection.

You are now the bridge, the ladder, from Earth to the Heavens, the Cosmos.

Feel your central channel, where your chakras meet, opening wider, to receive more flowing energy from the Heavens through you to the Earth, and back up to the Heavens.

Continue with your long deep breathing, feeling brighter and brighter light flowing through your crown, circling your auric field and down through your entire body, touching every cell, flowing into the Earth and back up.

Continue to experience this connection and flow…….

Feel your heart chakra opening to greater and greater volumes of light, filling with gratitude and love.

Continue to experience this opening and growing gratitude and love…….

Completely relax every cell in your body, bathing in light.

Ask for your highest light guides and guardians to be present, as your witnesses, as you receive the gift of Reiki.

REIKI ATTUNEMENT

Through the act of receiving an attunement, initiation, or empowerment from a Reiki Master Teacher, one's ability to channel infinite healing energy from Divine source is opened to greater capacity. This energy flows through the Teacher's connection to Divine source, through their heart, hands and into the student's energetic body.

The flow of light healing energy reboots the energetic fields of the student, raising their vibration. This can be seen as upgrading your personal software from Word 2000 to Word 2007. Your personal energetic system, residing within and around your body, gets re-wired, upgraded to operate at a higher vibration. The higher one raises their vibration, the higher levels of consciousness are more accessible.

At the time of your attunement, you also receive a Reiki guide, a higher vibrational light being, that assists you in your Reiki practice. You are now a Level 1 Reiki practitioner.

Receiving an attunement, raising your vibration, may take some time to integrate through your physical, emotional, mental, and spiritual bodies. Always remember, you are in charge of your own personal energetic dial. On days when you feel you are having too many energetic downloads or running too much energy, turn down your dial. On days when you feel you are ready for more, turn your dial up. Daily practice continues to strengthen your connection and ability to flow higher levels of light energy.

When you begin, it's similar to being a 110 extension cord, plugging into Divine, highest light energy. As you adjust to this new vibration and you use your Reiki daily, you will be ready to become a 220 extension cord. As you grow and adjust into this energy, you will become a 440 extension cord. Until finally one day, you realize that your connection is infinite, all around you, is part of you, and you are a being of light. You live and flow through the energy with every step and every breath you take. Why would you ever turn it off? Some people receive a Reiki attunement and never use the energy. Like any unexercised muscle, the Reiki will still be there, but will be weak. A Level 1 Reiki practitioner who uses the energy daily will be much stronger and more powerful than a Reiki Master who never uses the energy.

It's possible to get what we call a Reiki headache or other flu-like symptoms from running so much energy as you raise your vibration. Use your dial to adjust the flow of energy. Take the time to integrate new levels of consciousness and vibration at a pace that is comfortable.

As you release congested energy throughout your chakras, other physical areas may show up with discomfort. Healing energetically can be compared to peeling off the layers of an onion. As you peel the first layer, the toxins are released. And so it is with each layer afterwards. As you release, Reiki energy allows you to heal at each level. Be kind, loving, and gentle to yourself as you go through this process. This process can also be compared to the lotus flower. The root of the lily pad is deep in the dark, muddy bottom of the pond. The roots send up the shoots through the murkiness, until the light is reached. The lily pad grows on top of the fluidity of the water. As the combination of the nutrients from the mud, murky water, and the light blend together, a lotus blossom begins to form. Eventually the blossom unfolds into magnificent beauty, as do we.

Remember to drink lots of water daily. As you run more energy processing and filling, you dehydrate. Electrolytes or lemon can be added daily to your water intake. Nurturing our physical body as we heal our mental, emotional, and spiritual bodies is important, as they are all connected.

Feeling the Flow of Reiki Energy

After your actual attunement, it is important to give yourself time to feel and integrate the attunement process and the new energetic connection that you have received. Many students find it helpful to write down their experience and feelings. This may take 10 to 15 minutes.

Exercise to Feel the Energy

Rub your hands together and feel them become warm. Now cup your hands into a ball. Start to lightly pulsate your hands, back and forth, and feel the energy building between them. Once this energy becomes very strong, separate your hands a few inches apart, and continue to pulsate. Once the energy becomes very strong in this position, widen the spread between your hands further. Keep your fingers together and your hands slightly curved, like holding a ball. Keep this position with your fingers and hands as you practice Reiki.

By maintaining this position, your hands are able to flow greater volumes of energy. Keep pulsating your hands a little further apart, until you are shoulder width apart. Do you still feel the energy? Continue to slowly widen your arms, still pulsing and feeling the energy between your hands. Now, as far as you can spread your arms, hands still facing each other and pulsing. Close your eyes and feel the energy between your hands. Envision the energy filling your auric field. Relax your arms down to your lap. Feel the energy streaming through your crown, pulsating all around your auric field, throughout your body and down to your feet. This is a continual flow of light healing energy that is with you 24/7. This energy will grow daily, as long as you activate your Reiki. It will vibrate through and off of your body, affecting everything and everyone around you in a positive manner!

Separate into pairs. Face your partner. One of you is the receiver and one of you is the sender. The receiver sits comfortably, with hands on thighs, palms up and eyes closed. The sender leans forward and places cupped hands lightly on the receiver's knees. Eyes closed, crown chakra open, and flow the Reiki energy into your partner's knees. The touch is so light, like a butterfly landing. Do this for a few minutes. The sender disconnects and sits back. Repeat this exercise, trading positions with your partner. Once completed, each student shares the receiving and sending experience with the class.

Everyone return to their seats. Now we will focus on one student at a time. This student sits comfortably, with their palms facing up on their thighs. The rest of the class places their hands, palms cupped and facing outward, at their heart center. The intention is to now flow Reiki energy to the receiver. Do this flow for a few minutes. Go around the room until everyone has had a turn to receive. Once completed, each student shares the receiving and sending experience with the class.

Everyone stand up and do a few aura strengthening exercises, drink water and walk around.

Fig. 1. Eyes

Fig. 2. Ears

Fig. 3. Crown

Fig. 4. Throat and Heart

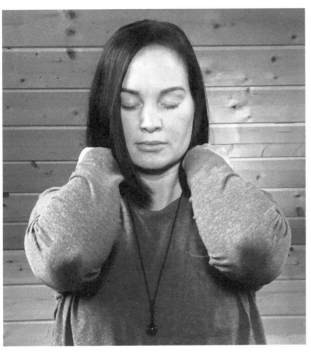

Fig. 5. Neck

(Same - Side view)

Fig. 6. Solar Plexus

Fig. 7. Sacral

Fig. 8. Root

Fig. 9. Mouth of Spirit

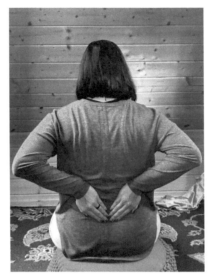

Fig. 10. Sacral

Fig. 11. Root

Fig. 12. Knees - anterior

Fig. 13. Knees - posterior

Fig. 14. Flowing

Fig. 15. Feet and Ankles

(Same - modified posture)

Fig. 16. Ankles

Fig. 17. Insoles

REIKI SESSION

Preparing to give a Reiki Session

Self preparation is very important before giving a Reiki session. This involves meditation, activation, and intention. Activate your Reiki. Bring your hands together, palms touching, to your heart, fingers pointing up and thumbs against your heart center. In Usui Reiki, this is called *Gassho*. Either repeat the Reiki ideals or choose your own words of honor, gratitude, and intention. Do this for five to 20 minutes every day. Opening your crown chakra, flow divine energy through your third eye, throat, heart, shoulders, elbows,, and palms. Feel the Reiki energy building in your palms. Focus on the Reiki energy. When all thoughts are dissolved and the flow of energy is all that is present, you are ready to flow Reiki to yourself or others.

When you are ready to give an actual Reiki session, repeat the Gassho meditation for one to two minutes above the recipient. During the meditation, ask for the Reiki energy to flow for the highest good of body, mind, emotions, or spirit of the recipient. Move your hands upward from your heart so that your thumbs rest on your third eye. Ask for highest light guidance to assist you in this session. Guide your hands, flowing the Reiki energy, to best treat the recipient's needs. This technique is called *Reiki-ho*, or *indication of the spirit*, as defined by Usui Sensei. At this time, also invite any Highest Light Guide, Guardian, Ascended Master, Archangel, or ancestor that the spirit of this recipient feels supported by or safe with, to be present. Also remember, your Reiki guide is present to assist.

Reiki guidance and intuition have now made you ready to flow a Reiki treatment or session. Usui Sensei referred to this action as *Chiryo*. Following the intelligence of the energy and guided intuition, your hands will flow to the areas needed to assist in creating balance in the recipient.

Detecting the flow of energy

Now that you have prepared yourself for the Reiki session, it is time to detect the flow of energy in the client. Usui Sensei used a method called *Byosen Scanning*. The meaning of Byosen is *dis-ease line*. To detect the flow of energy, start at either the head or the feet of the recipient, and place your hands barely above their body. Slowly move the length of the body, noticing any sensations in your hands or body. The sensations can be hot, cold, tingly, sharp, etc. Any of your senses can be activated. You may experience a sensation of seeing, hearing, feeling, tasting, or smelling as your hands flow over their body. Repeat this movement through each layer of the auric field, noticing any difference between layers.

Giving a Reiki session

After you have detected and felt the flow of energy, or the areas of congested energy, you are ready to begin the session. Allow the Reiki intelligence and Divine guidance to guide your hands to work in the areas that they are needed. As the energy shifts, allow your hands to flow, be guided, to the next area. Remember, this can be through any level of the auric field or by actually touching the body. The touch is light, like a butterfly. Sensations that you experience are most likely guidance being given to you to assist in the healing. Your personal will and ego are set aside. You are the instrument to flow the Reiki light energy to the recipient. You do not know their highest good. You cannot be attached to the outcome. The recipient's spirit will use the energy for their highest good at that moment. Some are ready to heal completely. Some only want a small amount of healing for the moment. It is their choice. Some need to learn a lesson or heal karma by experiencing their dis-comfort or dis-ease. The Reiki energy can assist in healing their body, emotions, mind, or spirit, so they can find peace and comfort. Their journey is unique and only their spirit knows what is needed. If the recipient is willing to process, forgive, release, and fill with light and unconditional love, they will heal. This can take one session or many. Empowering the recipient with self-love and higher spiritual connection can assist them on their journey. They co-create their wellness, their wholeness.

Closing and Cleansing at the end of a session

Upon the completion of the session, it is essential to close the recipient's chakras and auric field. Holding one of your hands above their crown chakra, take your other hand and scoop the energy up from below their feet to meet your other hand. Repeat this three times, with the intention of grounding the energy and connecting and balancing their chakras and auric field. Holding your arms wide, slowly bring the energy together by bringing your hands together over their power center. This movement is like zipping, sealing in the energy.

Bring your hands to your third eye. Say words of gratitude for all of those who were present to assist you and the flow of the Reiki energy. Move your hands to your heart. Slowly bow in honor and respect to the person on the table. Step back and cut the energetic ties that you have had during the session.

It is important upon the completion of a Reiki session to remove your energetic attachment to the recipient. This can be a person, animal, plant, location, etc. After the session is over, the blessing and respect having been given, step back from the recipient. Removing your energetic tie is necessary. This can be done in various ways. Intention is needed for separation. Physically you can perform detaching with a few different techniques.

Place your hands on opposite shoulders by crossing your arms and slowly allow your hands to slide down your arms. Turn your hands once they reach your elbows, to slide down your forearms and through your hands, with the cutting, disengaging motion. Do this three times.

The intention while doing this motion is that you are disengaging the energy that was flowing through your body, through your hands, to the recipient. This motion can also be done one arm and hand at a time, repeating three times. You can also detach by washing your hands and shaking them vigorously, with the intention of disengaging. This allows the recipient to leave, or be left in their own energetic field, filled and sealed with the Reiki energy, without energetic ties to you. This action also allows you to be refreshed and energetically clear.

The cutting or disengaging motion can also be used at any time during the day or night when you feel you have been exposed to negative energy or psychic attack. Employees who work in toxic environments can use this technique often. It is comforting and empowering to be able to cut and disengage after a negative phone call, comment in a meeting, or just being inside a toxic building all day. Cutting and leaving the work energy at work, as soon as you walk out the door to go home, allows you to arrive home energetically clean.

To remove unwanted energy from an object or space, your intention must be clear. With the Reiki energy activated, flow the light vibration into and around the object or space you wish to cleanse. Continue to flow the energy until you feel a shift in sensation or vibration. Sometimes this is a "knowing". Upon completion, disengage and use the cutting motion around yourself and the object or area/space. Cleansing objects before bringing them into your home or office is a good idea. Any healing tools such as crystals, feathers, etc., benefit from a cleansing after they have assisted in a session.

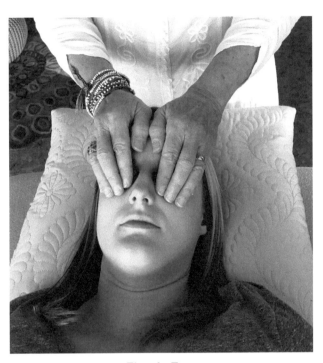

Fig. 1. Eyes

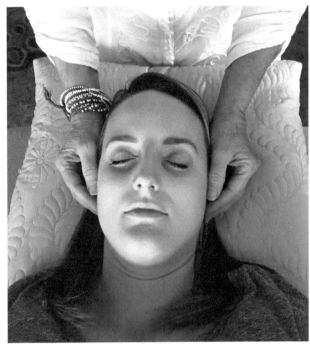

Fig. 2. Ears

Fig. 3. Crown

Fig. 4. Mouth of Spirit

Fig. 5. Heart

Fig. 6. Shoulders

Fig. 7. Throat

(Same - angled view)

Fig. 8. Shoulder

Fig. 9. Shoulder/Elbow

Fig. 10. Shoulder/Hand

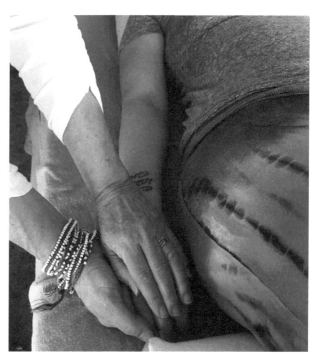

Fig. 11. Hand

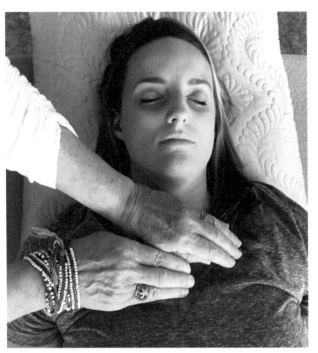

Fig. 12. Heart/Thyroid

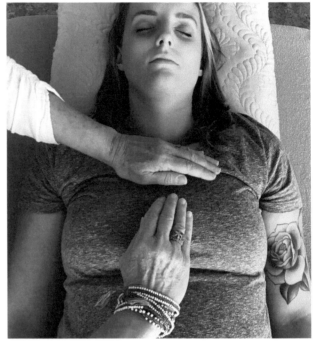

(Same - alternate hand placement)

Fig. 13. Solar Plexus

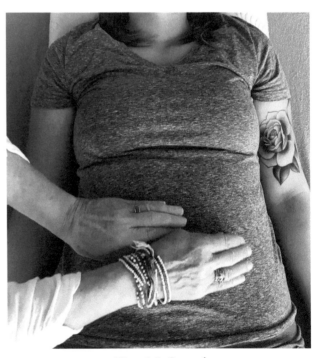

Fig. 14. Sacral

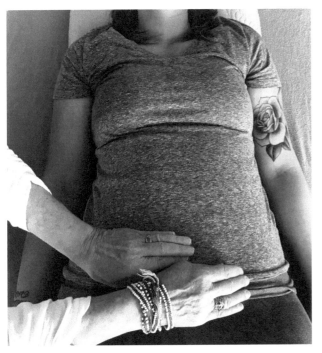

Fig. 15. Root

(Same - hand placement for modesty)

Fig. 16. Hip

Fig. 17. Knee

(Same - alternate hand placement)

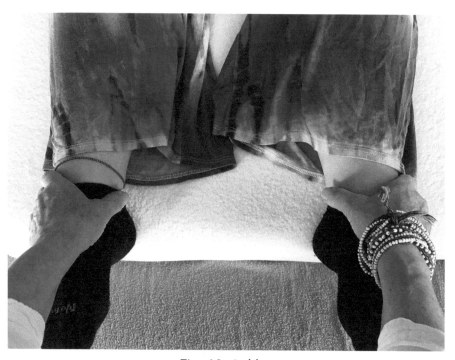

Fig. 18. Ankles

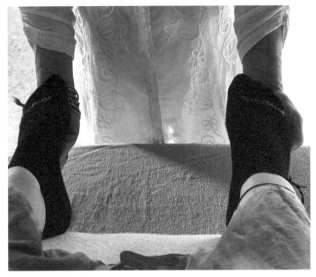

Fig. 19. Feet

(Same - alternate hand placement)

Fig. 20. Connecting shoulder
to hip energy

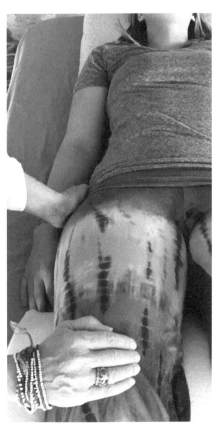

Fig. 21. Connecting hip
to knee energy

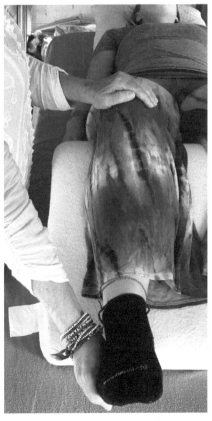

Fig. 22. Connecting knee
to foot energy

For following positions, gently instruct subject to turn face-down.
Provide assistance when appropriate.

Fig. 23. Mouth of Spirit

Fig. 24. Base of Neck

Fig. 25. Shoulders

Fig. 26. Heart

Fig. 27. Solar Plexus

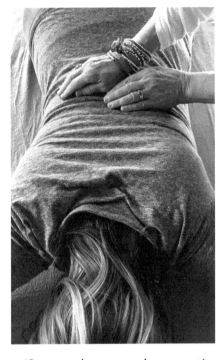

(Same - alternate placement)

Fig. 28. Sacral

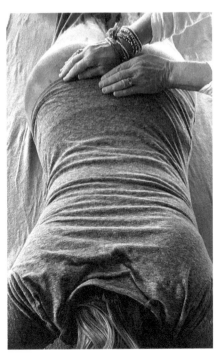

Fig. 29. Root

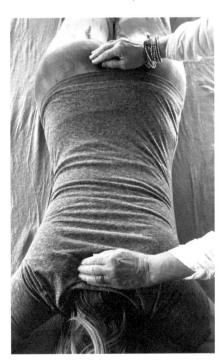

Fig. 30. Connecting neck
to root

Fig. 31. Knees

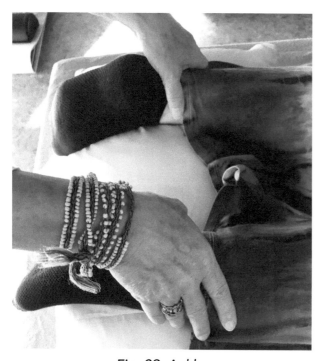

Fig. 32. Ankles

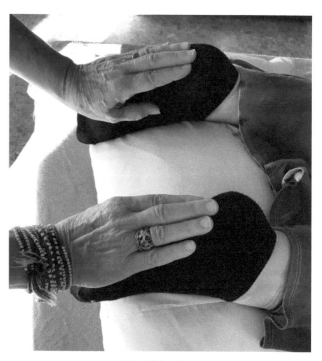

Fig. 33. Feet

SEATED REIKI
Hand Placement
1 / 3

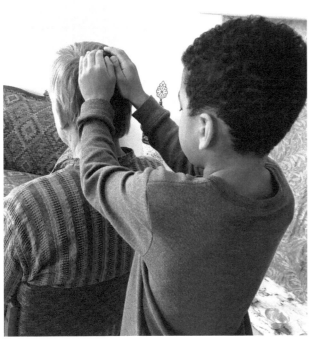

Fig. 1. Crown

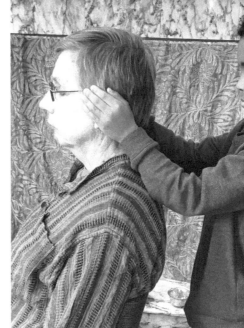

Fig. 2. Ears

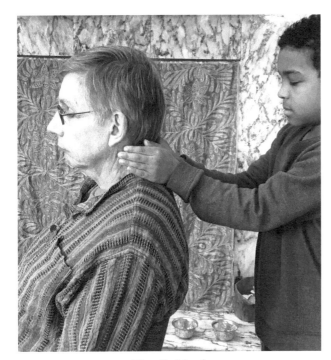

Fig. 3. Neck

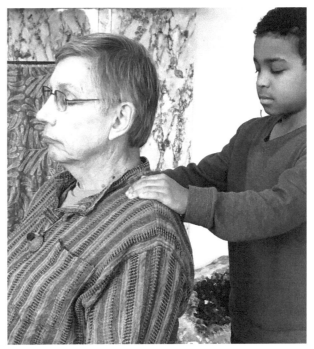

Fig. 4. Shoulders

Fig. 5. Heart

Fig. 6. Shoulder to Hand

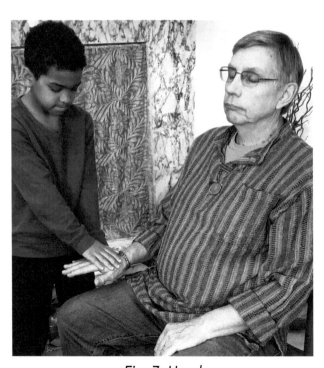

Fig. 7. Hand

Fig. 8. Knees

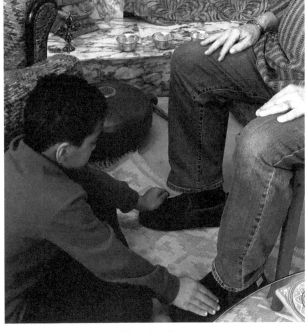

Fig. 9. Feet

ANATOMY FOR REIKI - FRONT VIEW

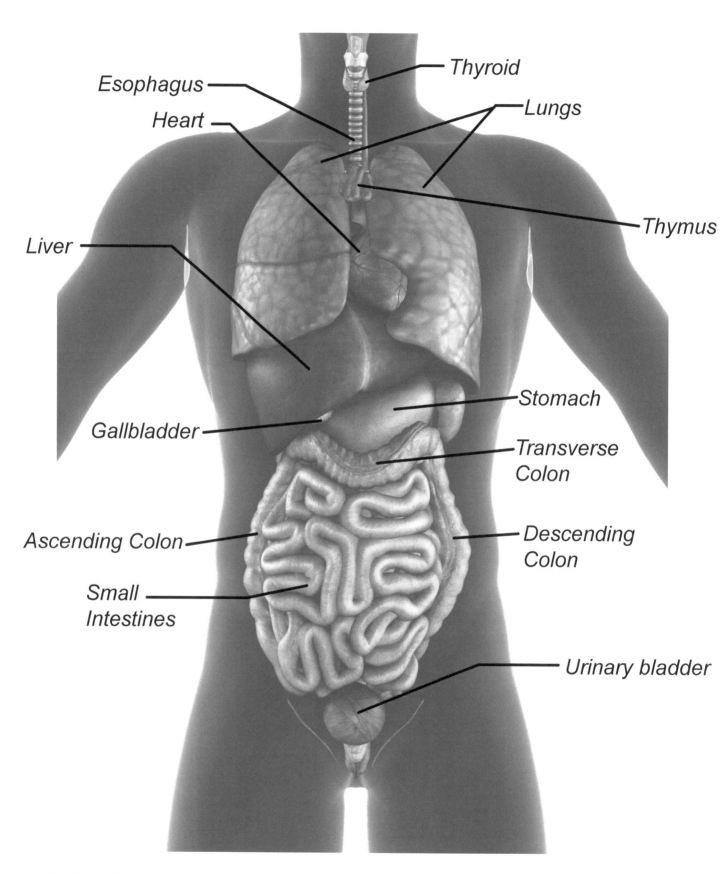

Esophagus

Thyroid

Heart

Lungs

Thymus

Liver

Stomach

Gallbladder

Transverse Colon

Ascending Colon

Descending Colon

Small Intestines

Urinary bladder

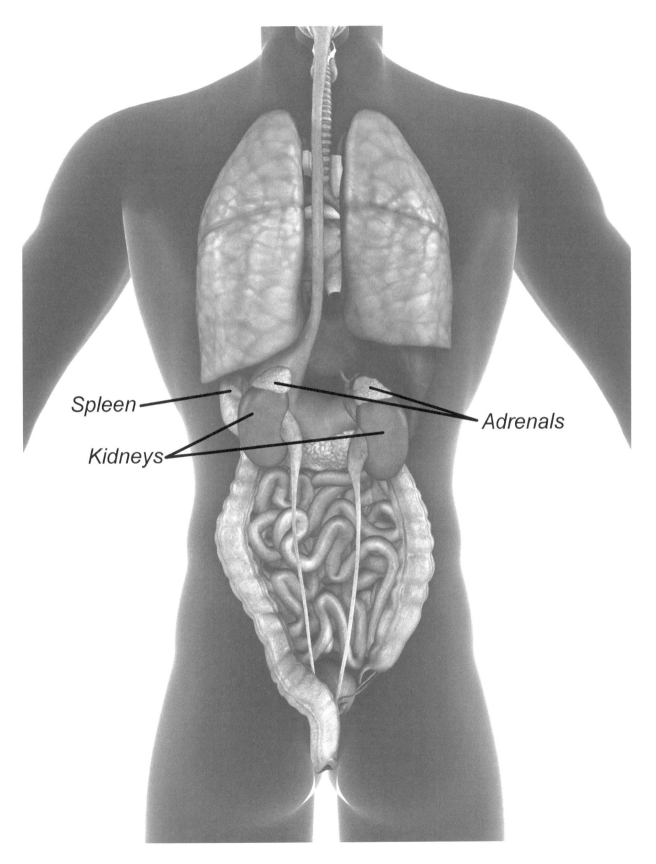

Spleen

Adrenals

Kidneys

CLIENT INFORMATION FORM

I understand that Reiki is a simple, gentle, hands-on energy technique that is used for stress reduction and relaxation. I understand that Reiki practitioners do not diagnose conditions nor do they prescribe or perform medical treatment, prescribe substances, nor interfere with the treatment of a licensed medical professional. It is recommended that I see a licensed physician or licensed health care professional for any physical or psychological ailment I may have.

I understand and believe that the body has the ability to heal itself, and to do so complete relaxation is often beneficial. I also understand that multiple treatments may be necessary to bring my system back into balance.

Privacy Notice:

No information about any client will be discussed or shared with any third party without the written consent of the client or parent/guardian if the client is under the age of 18.

Name: (Please Print)_____ DOB_____

Home Phone: _____ Cell Phone:_____

Address: _____

City, State, Zip:_____

Email:_____

Emergency Contact:_____Phone:_____

Are you currently under the care of a physician? ❑ Yes ❑ No
Have you ever had a Reiki session before? ❑ Yes ❑ No
Are you sensitive to perfumes or fragrances? ❑ Yes ❑ No
Are you sensitive to touch? ❑ Yes ❑ No
Are you on prescription medication? ❑ Yes ❑ No

Do you have any areas of concern?_____

_____

Signed:_____ Date:_____

Parent/Guardian consent if client is under 18 _____

DAILY PRACTICE

Take five, 10, 15, 20 or more minutes, whatever you can give, to start your day calm and balanced. Remember, it takes 40 days to establish a new pattern of behavior!

Activate your Reiki

Activate your Reiki upon waking up! I never turn mine off, but ask that it be activated 24/7. However, I believe showing gratitude and saying the name of Reiki adds strength to the energy.

Balance your Chakras with the Chakra meditation.

Aura Strengthening

Start every morning with this exercise, as soon as your feet hit the floor!
Repeat as many times as day as needed. At work, fellow employees think you are just stretching out, so do it without worry. Teach it to your friends at work, too. And don't forget to cut, cut, cut away unwanted energy that you are exposed to.

Recite your affirmations

Usui Sensei gave us the example of the five precepts. You can use these or create your own. Use your voice!

Breath

Breath is sacred. It is our life force that flows through every cell of our body. In many cases, traumatic life experiences and stress, no matter what creates it, has taken our breath away. Taking the time to re-train our breath to be full and rich, takes daily practice. Sometimes, moment to moment practice is needed. For ourselves, doing the chakra meditation every morning, and/or during the day, can help keep us balanced, relieve stress and relieve minor physical discomfort.

To self-empower family, friends and others, teach them!
Take the time to take a very long deep breath, up from the bottoms of the feet, all the way up through the body, reaching the top of the head. Exhale out any stress or tightness, nice and slow. Repeat this five times. If the tightness or stress is extreme, blow it out forcefully, with the intention of releasing the stress NOW! This breath can calm and balance immediately. Repeat this breath many times a day, as needed. Relieving stress and minor physical discomfort by breathing is free, has no side effects, and can never be done too much!

Teach this breath technique to everyone you share Reiki with. Start every Reiki session you give with this breath. As they leave a session, remind them to practice the calming breath daily.

Blessing your food and water with Reiki

What we put into our bodies has a direct effect on our bodies: physical, emotional, mental, or Spiritual. Most of the time, we are in control of what we expose ourselves to, as far as food, medicine, liquids, and water are concerned. The choice and purity of those items are personal. Granted, the quality of our choices directly affects our systems. What we can be aware of is this: Reiki energy can purify, cleanse, and bless whatever it is we are about to ingest.

Quick experiment: Fill two glasses of water from your kitchen faucet. Let one sit on the counter. Place your cupped hand over the second glass, running Reiki with the intention to purify, for 30 seconds. Smell and partially drink the untouched glass first. Wait a minute. Smell and partially drink the glass infused with Reiki. Amazing difference! Why would you not infuse Reiki into everything you eat and drink and offer to others! Don't forget your pet's food and water too!

Reiki your home and office

Fill your home and office with the intentions of love, light, and protection. Daily infusions of the Reiki energy build, like charging a battery. Each infusion strengthens and amplifies the Reiki energy. Everything will benefit from the higher vibration. Your pets, houseplants, anyone in your space, and the space itself feels the comfort and love.

Those who do not resonate or who wish harm, soon cannot enter your space, or if they do, they don't stay long!

SACRED SPACE

Setting aside a sacred space for yourself at home is extremely important. This can be a room, a small section of a room, a chair in the corner of a room that only you use, your private space. Use this space as you begin your daily practice. In the space perhaps you can have an altar, for your sacred pieces, that no one else touches. This can be a small table, a chest, a drawer, something that houses, protects, and honors your personal items. As you begin and end your day, use your sacred space. This space allows you to tune in to your highest good body, mind, emotions, and spirit. Light a small candle each morning, to represent and honor your light for the day. (Be sure to blow out, or put where no harm can be done if left. Small tea lights are perfect for this, as they only last two hours) Activate your Reiki. Do your affirmations, Gassho meditation, and aura strengthening. Whatever time you have, five minutes to whatever time you develop for this practice. You are worth every second of this time! It takes 40 days to establish a new pattern of behavior. If you make it to 38 and skip a day, you must start over. After 40 days, this practice becomes part of what you do, without even thinking about not doing it. It will be like leaving the house without brushing your hair or teeth.

Sacred space can also be a private, secluded place in nature where you can connect to your highest good. You can go to this place in your mind when the weather or time does not allow you to physically be there.

As part of your daily practice, honoring the seven directions and elements is important. This practice is ancient, has been and is practiced by many worldwide. Setting a circle of intention and protection daily grounds and connects your spirit and your journey. The significance of the directions may vary with different cultures. Research and read other interpretations to find the one that resonates with you.

The following is one belief system: Calling in the grandmothers and grandfathers and guardians of highest good in each of the following directions, create a sacred circle of honor and protection. The North represents the mother Earth and abundance. The East represents the air and the ability to see from higher perspective. The South represents fire and transformation. The West represents water, sustainer and giver of life on this planet. Each of these directions can have an animal totem representing the energy and also a color. Now, the direction of above representing highest consciousness, Great Spirit. The direction of below, as above, so below, highest consciousness. The final direction is found within Self. We are each the final direction. Now, you are ready to greet the day!

REIKI CIRCLE

As a new Level 1 Reiki Practitioner, daily practice on self is important to continue to raise and strengthen your Reiki energy. Practicing on your family members, pets, plants, etc., is valuable and beneficial to all.

Joining or building a Reiki Community in your area is energetically rewarding and strengthening. Finding like-minded people with similar practices is comforting. We all learn from each other. Practicing with others, outside of family members, can be a huge learning experience and very different. Each person and each session may present new ways the Reiki energy heals. Remember: we are clear and open channels for the Reiki energy to flow to the recipient for their highest good of body, emotions, mind, and spirit. We are not attached to the outcome of their healing, as we do not know their highest good.

Reiki circles can be formed several different ways.

If you have multiple Practitioners, we have found it best to work one on one, or no more than two Practitioners performing the Reiki on the recipient. This means having several tables, if multiple Practitioners are present. If there are others without tables, chair Reiki can be done. Others can hold the group in Reiki energy domes of light.

Some Reiki Circles are open to the public. They can be done in your home (if you are comfortable) or at an office, or public meeting room that allows gatherings. These Circles can be offered for free or for a minimal fee.

We offer regular, monthly Reiki Circles as ongoing education. All Reiki students, all levels, are invited to attend. Everyone has the opportunity to receive, give, and share. Questions are answered. New information is offered. This can be the only opportunity some Practitioners have to work with others.

Many layers of healing can be experienced and discussed. Everyone benefits and grows in their personal practice and understanding of Reiki. A monthly "tune up" is experienced. There is a minimal fee charged.

PRACTICE, PRACTICE, PRACTICE!!!

Never minimize the healing energy of Reiki.

Daily embrace greater volumes of infinite, Divine, unconditional love.

Domesticated Animal Chakras

Crown Chakra
Brow Chakra
Throat Chakra
Heart Chakra
Solar Plexus Chakra
Sacral Chakra
Root Chakra

ANIMAL REIKI

Over the years, many students have come to take Reiki classes specifically to train and use Reiki with their pets. Aging pet issues, adopted animals that were abused, animals with phobias, and to bring calmness to veterinary clinics, are just a few examples of people using Reiki with animals.

Using Reiki, several students have been able to relieve pain and increase the quality of life in their elderly pets. My own cat lived to be 22 years old. She was in excellent health until her last six months, when her body finally began to give out with age. She was an amazing Reiki cat, and would often accompany me in private sessions for cat lovers. My dogs lived to be 16, 17, and 18 years old with good health until their passing. They too loved to be around Reiki sessions for others. Animals love and respond to Reiki.

Reiki can be used with any animal, bird, reptile, fish, etc., domesticated or wild, tiny or huge. A friend sits on her deck at her cabin in the forest and sends Reiki out, in a radiant bubble, surrounding the area. Not only does the forest and everything living in it receive this compassionate healing light, but it is common for deer, birds, and squirrels to come forward. Eagles are constant visitors. All receive and respond to the vibrational Reiki energy filled with love.

Clients call for house visits for their pets. They also text or email me a picture of their pet that is in need of healing energy. Animals can receive Reiki with hands-on or long distance. Either way is effective with the animal client. The Reiki requests are for unlimited reasons: injuries, phobias, old age, chronic or temporary pain, inflammation, lost, stress, fear, everything humans experience! Animals are extremely tuned in to vibration and are very sensitive to Reiki energy. They have no belief systems getting in their way of receiving unconditional, compassionate, comforting, vibrational energy.

It is important to remember that, like people, you ask permission of the animal to touch them. Animals communicate with pictures, through telepathy. Send Reiki energy as you approach, or sit in a dome of the energy and let them come to you. In your mind, see pure love flowing from your heart to them for the comfort they need.

Reiki with Your Own Pet

As a Reiki Practitioner, hopefully you are filling your house daily with the Reiki energy. This way, everything in your house is already adjusting to and receiving the healing, compassionate vibration. When you actually want to give your pet a Reiki session, sit down and start beaming the Reiki energy. Picture in your mind your pet receiving the energy. If they want to come close, they will. Often times, the pet will actually put the area of discomfort into your hands. They will sit or lay by you or in your lap. Sometimes they may keep some distance, but remain in the room. Honor their choice. Continue to bathe them in the Reiki energy until they signal completion. They will either walk away, giving distance, leave the room, or perhaps tell you with a look or action. It is possible that your hands will cease to flow the energy, showing you the session is complete. Seal the light energy into their auric field and ask for it to continue to flow and bring healing for your pet's highest good. Show gratitude.

At times, your pet will come to you and ask for the Reiki energy. Being aware and willing to flow Reiki energy when needed or asked for is a gift to everyone in your house.

Reiki House Calls

When a client has called you to come to their dwelling to give their pet Reiki, it is important to start sending the energy as soon as you make the appointment. Have the client send, text, or email a picture of the animal who is to receive the session. Send Reiki as you are driving to the address. Keep the picture of the animal in your mind and pure love in your heart, sending Reiki as you drive. The animal is already receiving the healing vibration. By the time you arrive, the pet is ready to receive. As you walk into the room with the pet, continue to fill the room with Reiki energy. Sit comfortably on a couch or floor, depending on the size of the animal. Radiate pure love and light Reiki energy through every cell of your body. The pet may stay a distance away. Eventually, they will make their way closer and closer until they are beside you, in your lap, or have placed part of their body in your hands. Continue to flow the energy. When the pet has had enough, they will shift in some manner or walk away. The session is over. Seal the light energy in their auric field and ask for it to continue to flow and bring healing for the pet's highest good. Show gratitude upon leaving.

Reiki in Nature

We can send Reiki energy to anything and everything in nature. Sitting quietly and with intention, envision a dome emanating from your body, filled with pure love and healing for whatever species want to receive. The dome can be any size. Open your crown chakra to allow greater volumes of Divine light energy to flow through your heart and every cell of your body. Upon completion, seal the energy in the area and ask for it to continue to bring healing of highest good. Show gratitude upon leaving.

BIBLIOGRAPHY

Bruyere, Rosalyn L. *Wheels of Light: Chakras, Auras, and the Healing Energy of the Body.*
    New York, NY: Fireside, 1994. Print

Dale, Cyndi. *New Chakra Healing: The Revolutionary 32-Center Energy System.*
    St. Paul, MN: Llewellyn Publications, 1998. Print.

Doi, Hiroshi. *Iyashino Gendai Reiki-ho: Modern Reiki Method for Healing.*
    Coquitlam, British Columbia: Fraser Journal Publishing, 2000. Print.

Eden, Donna. *Energy Medicine: Balancing Your Body's Energies for Optimal Health, Joy and Vitality*
    London, England: Penguin Group, 2008. Print.

Emoto, Masaru. *The Hidden Messages in Water.* Trans. David A Thayne.
    New York, NY: Beyond Words Publishing, 2004. Print.

Gerber, Richard. *Vibrational Medicine: The #1 Handbook of Subtle-Energy Therapies.* Third Ed.
    Rochester, Vermont: Bear & Company, 2001. Print.

Govinda, Kalashatra. *A Handbook of Chakra Healing: Spiritual Practice for Health, Harmony, and Inner Peace.* Old Saybrook, CT: Konecky & Konecky, 2002. Print.

Hart, Francene. *Sacred Geometry of Nature: Journey on the Path of the Divine.*
    Rochester, Vermont: Bear & Company, 2017. Print

Judith, Anodea. *Wheels of Life: A User's Guide To The Chakra System.*
    Woodbury, MN: Llewellyn Publications, 2010. Print.

Khalsa, Dharma Singh and Cameron Stauth. *Meditation as Medicine: Activate The Power Of Your Natural Force.* New York: Simon & Schuster, Inc. 2001. Print.

Lee, Ilchi. *Healing Chakra: Light to Awaken My Soul.* Sedona, AZ: Healing Society. 2005. Print.

Lubeck, Walter and Frank Arjava Petter and William Lee Rand. *The Spirit of Reiki: The Complete Handbook of the Reiki System.* Twin Lakes, WI: Lotus Press. 2009. Print.

Miller, Jessica A. *Reiki's Birthplace: A Guide To Kurama Mountain.*
    Sedona, AZ: Infinite Light Healing Studies Center, Inc. 2006. Print.

Orloff, Judith. *Intuitive Healing: 5 Steps To Physical, Emotional, and Sexual Wellness.*
New York, NY: Random House, Inc. 2000. Print.

Pond, David. *Chakras For Beginners: A Guide to Balancing Your Chakra Energies.*
Woodbury, MN: Llewellyn Publications, 2009. Print.

Rand, William Lee. *Reiki For A New Millennium.* Southfield, MI: Vision Publications, 1998. Print.

Rand, William Lee. *The Healing Touch: First and Second Degree Manual.*
Southfield, MI: Vision Publications, 2005. Print

Stein, Diane. *Essential Reiki: A Complete Guide to an Ancient Healing Art.*
Berkeley, CA: The Crossing Press, 1995. Print

Usui, Mikao and Frank Arjava Petter. *The Original Reiki Handbook of Dr. Mikao Usui.*
Twin Lakes, WI: Lotus Press, 2011. Print.

CPSIA information can be obtained
at www.ICGtesting.com
Printed in the USA
LVHW071025170219
607791LV00022B/1059/P